MATH PHONICS™
PRE-GEOMETRY

Quick Tips and Alternative Techniques for Math Mastery

BY MARILYN B. HEIN
ILLUSTRATED BY RON WHEELER

Teaching & Learning Company
1204 Buchanan St., P.O. Box 10
Carthage, IL 62321-0010

THIS BOOK BELONGS TO

_____

ACKNOWLEDGEMENTS

Sincere thanks to my sons, Adam and Nick, for their tech support and to my husband, Joe, for taking over the housework for a couple of weeks so I could finish this book!

DEDICATION

To my students who are always delightful: Jed Shepherd, Chrissie Truelove, Hanna Knolla, Hannah Holden, Britten Kuckelman, Maureen Ochs, Ashley Ryan and Jenna Donovan.

Cover art by Ron Wheeler

ISBN No. 1-57310-406-X

Printing No. 987654321

Teaching & Learning Company
1204 Buchanan St., P.O. Box 10
Carthage, IL 62321-0010

Math Phonics™ is a registered trademark to Marilyn B. Hein.

TABLE OF CONTENTS

Dear Teacher or Parent,

I had four major goals in mind while writing this book. I wanted to help beginning geometry students with:

1. understanding
2. memorizing
3. appreciating
4. enjoying

Here are some of the items that I think will aid students in *understanding* basic geometric concepts:

1. Metric rulers clearly marked with only one unit each.
2. Metric visual aids—soup cans, craft sticks and doorknobs—help kids remember metric units.
3. Paper cut-outs of solids for a math art project.
4. A 360° protractor printed right on one of the worksheets.
5. I.D. cards with the student's height in centimeters, cubic tissue boxes to teach volume and more.

How about *memorization*? Look at this:

1. Flash cards with solids and plane figures.
2. Vivid clue words related to polygons and metric units.
3. Bingo game to review knowledge about polygons.
4. A wall chart to stress the difference between pyramids and prisms.

What is there that can help students *appreciate* geometry?

1. Wall chart featuring geometric designs in nature.
2. Beautiful coloring design which can be found in the head of a daisy.
3. Word problems about different states in the U.S. Each problem relates some geometric concept to something that goes on in that state.

How about some *fun*?

1. A "magic circles" trick that students can try on friends or relatives.
2. Four coloring pages featuring geometric figures and designs.
3. Making solid shapes with plastic straws and paper clips.
4. Hexagon flowers made with two pencils and a paper clip.
5. Designs made on isometric dot paper . . . and more!

The worksheets are set up on four levels to offer choices to a teacher. Some classes might be ready to cover two levels in one year.

These pre-geometry lessons offer so many opportunities to relate math class to the real world—I sincerely enjoyed dreaming up all these ideas—and I sincerely hope you and your students will enjoy cooking up all these great projects!

Best wishes,

Marilyn

Marilyn B. Hein

WHAT IS MATH PHONICS™?

Math Phonics™ is a specially designed program for teaching math facts, skills and concepts initially or for remedial work.

WHY IS IT CALLED MATH PHONICS™?

In reading, phonics is used to group similar words, and it teaches the students simple rules for pronouncing each word.

In *Math Phonics*™, math terms and concepts are grouped and learned by means of clue words, mnemonic devices and hands-on activities. Abstract geometry concepts are related to real world objects and familiar words.

In reading, phonics develops mastery by repetitive use of words already learned.

Math Phonics™ uses repetition in the form of games, wall charts and review to reinforce students' understanding.

HOW WAS MATH PHONICS™ DEVELOPED?

Why did "Johnny" have so much trouble learning to read during the years that phonics was dropped from the curriculum of many schools in this country? For the most part, he had to simply memorize every single word in order to learn to read, an overwhelming task for a young child. If he had an excellent memory or a knack for noticing patterns in words, he had an easier time of it. If he lacked those skills, learning to read was a nightmare, often ending in failure–failure to learn to read and failure in school.

Phonics seems to help many children learn to read more easily. Why? When a young child learns one phonics rule, that one rule unlocks the pronunciation of dozens or even hundreds of words. It also provides the key to parts of many larger words. The trend in U.S. schools today seems to be to include phonics in the curriculum because of the value of that particular system of learning.

As a substitute teacher, I have noticed that math teacher manuals sometimes have some valuable phonics-like memory tools for teachers to share with students to help them memorize math facts–the addition, subtraction, multiplication and division facts which are the building blocks of arithmetic. However, much of what I remembered from my own education was not contained in the available materials. I decided to create my own materials based upon what I had learned during the past 40 years as a student, teacher and parent.

The name *Math Phonics*™ occurred to me because the tricks, patterns and memory techniques that I have assembled are similar to language arts phonics in several ways. Most of these tricks and clue words are short and easy to learn as are phonics rules. Phonics doesn't teach meanings or words or the more complex skills involved in writing. It merely teaches how to say the words. The skills can be taught later if students know how to read. *Math Phonics*™—*Pre-Geometry* does not teach how to develop a proof. It merely teaches the meanings of basic words and concepts. These can be used later to learn the more complex skills. Last of all, Math Phonics™ relies on lots of drill and review, just as language arts phonics does.

Students must master basic math facts and concepts and the sooner the better. When I taught seventh and eighth grade math over 30 years ago, I was amazed at the number of students who had not mastered the basic math facts and concepts. At that time, I had no idea how to help them. I was educated with a secondary education minor and my college math classes did not address these basic topics. I had not yet delved into my personal memory bank to try to remember how I had mastered those facts.

When some of our six children had problems with the basics, I was strongly motivated to give some serious thought to the topic. I knew my children had to master the basics, and I had to come up with additional ways to help them. The *Math Phonics*™ materials have worked so well that I have found that students not only do better in math, but enjoy more self-confidence in every way.

I have always marveled at the large number of people who tell me that they "hated math" when they were kids. I wonder how many of them struggled with the basics when they needed to have them clearly in mind. I firmly believe that a widespread use of *Math Phonics*™ could be a tremendous help in solving the problem of "math phobia."

WHAT ARE THE PRINCIPLES OF MATH PHONICS™?

There are three underlying principles of *Math Phonics*™.
They are: 1. Understanding
2. Learning
3. Mastery
Here is a brief explanation of the meaning of these principles.

1. **UNDERSTANDING:** All true mathematical concepts are abstract which means they can't be touched. They exist in the mind. For most of us, understanding such concepts is much easier if they can be related to something in the real world–something that can be touched and experienced.

    Thus I present ideas for demonstrating new concepts with hands-on activities—geometric shapes made of straws and paper clips, for example. Geometry is a part of *everything* in the world from daisy heads to the design of a jet plane. When a new concept is related to something familiar, the basic understanding comes more easily.

2. **LEARNING:** Once the basic understanding is in place, students must *learn* the new material in a way that keeps it in place next week, next month and next year. Here is where the clue words and objects in the classroom help students have a good mental image that they can remember.

3. **MASTERY:** We have all had the experience of memorizing some information for a test or quiz tomorrow and then promptly forgetting most of it. We want math students to retain what they have learned over the long term. *Math Phonics*™ provides wall charts, games and flash cards to accomplish this without the "drill and kill" problem.

HOW TO MAKE METRIC RULERS

1. Copy this page on tagboard.
2. Cut the rulers apart. A centimeter ruler can be found on Worksheet M (page 57).
3. Tape the sections of the rulers so the numbers are in order. Laminate or reinforce with tape.
4. Use these to discuss the metric system and measure various items.
5. Collect the meter rulers to use again.

Decimeter Ruler (10 dm = 1 meter)

9	10
7	8
5	6
3	4
1	2

Decimeters

Millimeter Ruler (1000 mm = 1 meter)

SUMMARY OF THE 10 BASIC STEPS

1. Solids

It's easier to start with solids than plane figures for pre-geometry students since solids can be touched. Students will describe, model, draw and classify solids and see how they are used in the world around us.

2. Plane Figures

Next we have the geometric figures which have no thickness. They can be studied by looking at items which have the same shape such as a flag (rectangle) and a checkerboard (square). Clue words and flash cards will help students remember the different polygons.

3. Points, Lines, Planes & Angles

Segments and rays are also included. Protractors will be introduced here and used again in Lesson Plan 7. Also included are right, acute and obtuse angles and perpendicular lines. We will not try to teach the idea that points, lines and planes have no size—that idea is a challenge even for adults. That can be learned later. It is an extremely abstract concept. Beginning students can learn geometric terms and concepts without worrying about that.

4. Metric System

The main goal of this section is to give students a firm, basic understanding of millimeter, centimeter, decimeter, meter and kilometer. Some excellent visual aids and clue words are included along with a few conversion problems. There is a Metric Unit Guide (page 52) which also covers hectometers and decameters. Students should keep this as a reference.

5. Perimeter & Circumference

This section includes radius and diameter. There is a simple demonstration regarding the value of pi. I do not remember seeing that demonstration while I was a student. I believe such demonstrations are very important in helping students understand and remember. There is a wall chart which explains how to find the area of a circle. See page 69. Students should keep a copy of this wall chart for future reference although the problems in this book do not cover the area of a circle.

6. Area & Volume

This section also stresses clear demonstrations and real-world examples.

7. Lines of Symmetry & Measuring Angles

These two concepts prepare students for understanding congruent triangles—the basis for many geometric proofs. Here, students will again use protractors.

8. Summary & Review

Hand this out so students can refer to it for a classroom review before the assessment.

9. Assessment

Here are four one-page assessments—one for each level in this book.

10. Answers

OBJECTIVES: For all four levels.

1. Describe, model, draw and classify geometric solids.
2. Discuss surfaces, edges and corners.
3. Relate geometric solids to the real world.
4. Use isometric dot paper to reproduce and enlarge plane and solid figures.

NOTE: Read the Math History below to the class. Students may research and write a brief report on these events for extra credit. Also, be sure each student has a Math Notebook. This can be a purchased three-prong pocket folder, or have students make one for a math art project. Directions for making a folder from a brown grocery bag can be found in *Math Phonics™—Multiplication*, page 7. Keep flash cards, worksheets, clue words, definitions, math spelling words and wall charts here.

MATH HISTORY: *Geometry* literally means "earth measure." The Egyptians gave us many of the early developments in geometry. They did measure the Earth after the annual flooding of the Nile to find land boundaries destroyed by the floods. Although they had only primitive tools, they built the pyramids with great precision. The Greeks reached some of the same conclusions as the Egyptians, but they were more interested in proving why something worked than in using it in the real world.

LEVEL 1: Use for third grade or as needed.

1. Introduce six solids.
2. Discuss flat and curved surfaces.

CLASSROOM PRESENTATION: Solids have thickness—plane figures do not. Bring models of the six solids to the classroom. Show flat and curved surfaces.

  sphere: tennis ball, etc., one curved surface
  hemisphere: orange cut in half, globe (Point out each hemisphere.) one curved, one flat surface
  cylinder: soup can or mailing tube, two flat, one curved surface
  cone: pointed ice cream cone, one flat, one curved surface
  cube: alphabet blocks, dice, sugar cubes, storage cube, Rubik's Cube™, six flat surfaces
  rectangular solid: shoe box, cereal box, six flat surfaces

A cube is a rectangular solid with all edges the same length.

TAKE-HOME: Two sets of flash cards are on page 12. The first six cards are for this lesson. The others are for Lesson 2. Place in a zip-type bag in the math folder to study at home or school. Have a class aid or volunteer check students verbally. Give points to students who can name all the solids correctly. Worksheet A, page 17.

WALL CHART: Enlarge, color and laminate one uncut set of Level 1 flash cards. Use it as a wall chart.

OPTIONAL: Math Spelling Test
Spelling words: sphere, hemisphere, cylinder, cone, cube, rectangular solid

PAPER CUT-OUTS: Solids for math or a math art project, pages 23-28. Show students surfaces, edges and corners. The Level 2 worksheet will ask for these to be counted.

LEVEL 2: Use for fourth grade or as needed. Review if needed.

1. Discuss polyhedrons—solid objects with flat sides.
2. Use isometric dot paper to draw shapes and enlarge them.
3. Discuss pyramids and prisms.

CLASSROOM PRESENTATION: Use Wall Chart 1, page 16, to discuss the difference between pyramids and prisms. Make the triangular prism, page 25, and the triangular pyramid, page 26, before class so students can see the difference.

Copy isometric dot paper, pages 19-20, onto overhead projection film or enlarge and laminate a page to demonstrate at the chalkboard. Demonstrate copying a shape and then making each side twice as long. Students count spaces not dots to double.

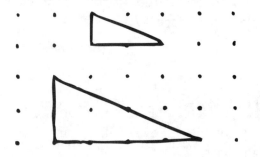

TAKE-HOME: Level 2 flash cards to keep in their math folders and study, page 14. The first two cards are for this lesson and the others are for Lesson Plan 2. If they do not have the Level 1 flash cards, pass those out, also. Give each student a set of paper cut-out models, pages 23-28. These can be used to count surfaces, edges and corners. Worksheet B, page 18. Isometric Dot Paper, page 19 or 20.

OPTIONAL: Triangular Prism from Straws, page 29. This can also be used to study surfaces, edges and corners.

OPTIONAL: Math Spelling Test
Spelling words: sphere, hemisphere, cube, cone, rectangular solid, cylinder, pyramid, prism

LEVEL 3: Use for fifth grade or as needed. Review if needed.

1. Recognize pyramids and prisms.
2. Define *polyhedrons* and *cylinders*.
3. Use isometric dot paper to draw a prism.

CLASSROOM PRESENTATION: Students will learn the definitions for *pyramids* and *prisms* in Level 4, but for Level 3, they need to recognize two different prisms and two different pyramids. A pyramid has triangular sides which meet at one point. See Wall Chart 1, page 16. A triangular pyramid also has a triangular base. A rectangular pyramid has a rectangular base. See page 26 for models of two types of pyramids. A prism has two congruent sides which can be any polygon. They are called the base and the top. The other sides are rectangles. See page 25 for two paper models.

DEFINITIONS: Students should memorize these:

cylinder: A solid object having two flat surfaces and one curved surface. (A soup can is an example.)

polyhedron: A solid object whose sides are flat surfaces. (Pyramids and prisms are both polyhedrons. *Poly* means "many" and *hedron* means "sides.")

TAKE-HOME: Give students Level 2 flash cards for these solids. Have students make paper cut-out models, pages 23-28, to help identify polyhedrons and cylinders. Discuss surfaces, edges and vertices—formerly called corners. Give points for learning flash cards and making cut-out models. Worksheet C, page 21 and dot paper, page 19 or 20.

OPTIONAL: Have students design prisms on isometric dot paper. They could have bases of hexagon, octagon, etc.

OPTIONAL: Math Spelling Test
Spelling words: cube, cylinder, cone, sphere, hemisphere, rectangular, triangular, pyramid, prism, polyhedron

LEVEL 4: Use for sixth grade or as needed. Review if needed.

1. Discuss the six geometric solids pictured on the Level 4 worksheet and their surfaces, edges and vertices (corners).
2. Define *pyramid* and *prism*.

CLASSROOM PRESENTATION: Review the six solids pictured on Level 4 worksheet. They are: rectangular prism, cylinder, rectangular pyramid, cone, triangular pyramid, triangular prism.

To distinguish between pyramids and prisms (Wall Chart 1, page 16):

1. First look for the triangles meeting at one point—that is the way to recognize a pyramid.
2. Look at the base of the pyramid. If it is a triangle, the pyramid is a triangular pyramid. The shape of the base names the pyramid.
3. If the solid has flat surfaces and is not a pyramid, it is a prism.
4. Find the base and top. If they are triangles, the solid is a triangular prism. The shape of the top and base name the prism.

DEFINITIONS: Have students memorize these:

pyramid: Solid shape with a polygon base and triangular sides which meet at one point.

prism: Solid shape with congruent polygon top and base and rectangular sides.

TAKE-HOME: Flash cards to study, page 14, paper cut-out models, pages 23-28. Give points for learning flash cards and making models. Then assign the worksheet, page 22, and a page of Isometric Dot Paper, page 19 or 20.

OPTIONAL: Math Spelling Test
Use words for Level 3.

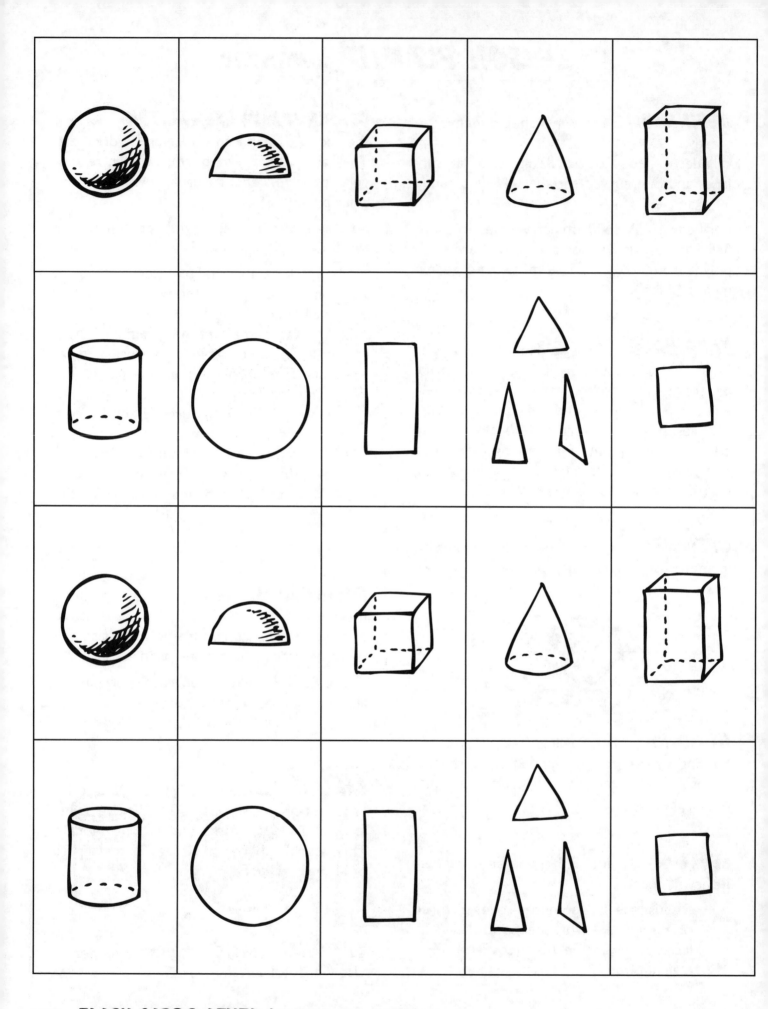

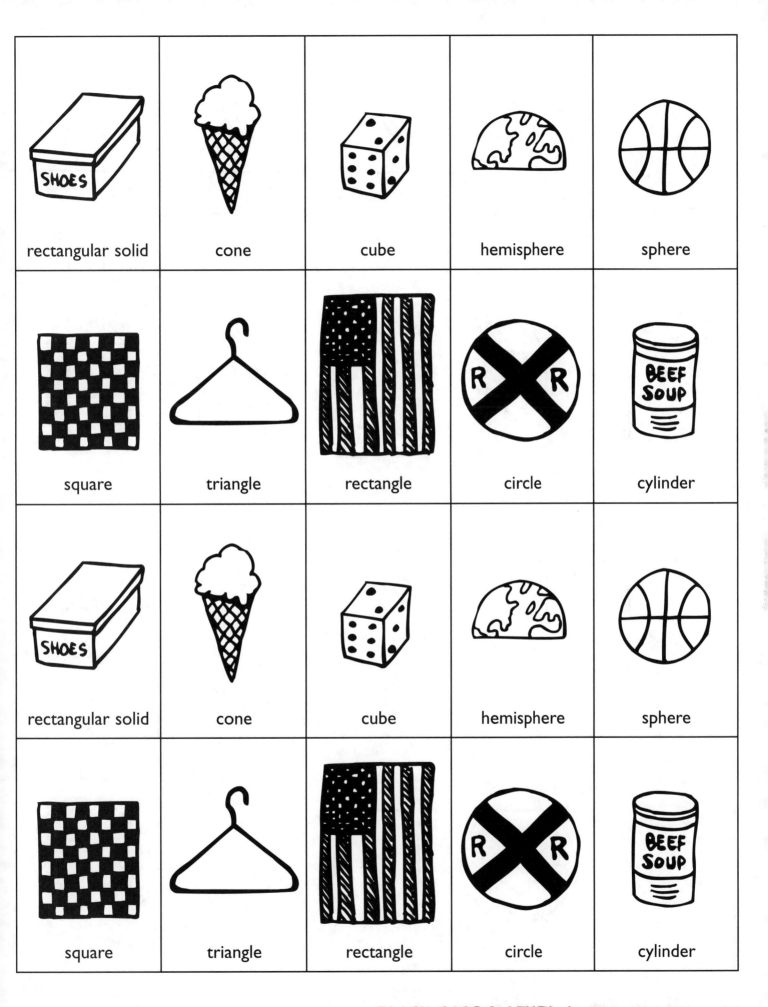

| rectangular solid | cone | cube | hemisphere | sphere |

| square | triangle | rectangle | circle | cylinder |

| rectangular solid | cone | cube | hemisphere | sphere |

| square | triangle | rectangle | circle | cylinder |

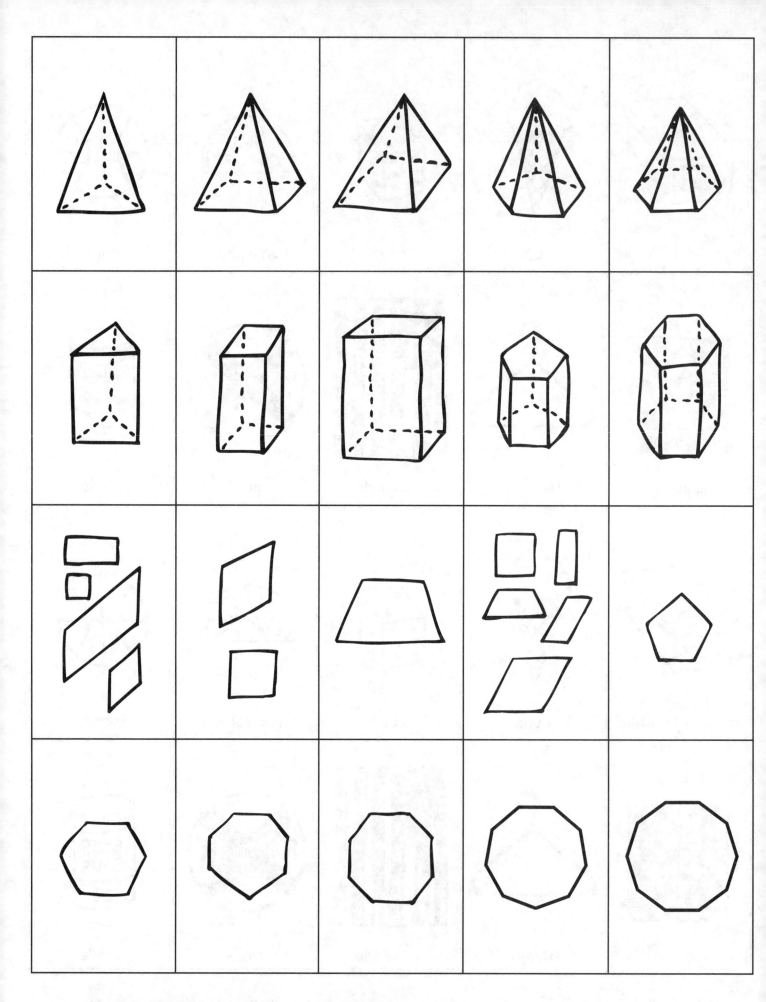

FLASH CARDS, LEVELS 2, 3 & 4 FRONT

hexagonal pyramid	pentagonal pyramid	rectangular pyramid	square pyramid	triangular pyramid
hexagonal prism	pentagonal prism	rectangular prism	square prism	triangular prism
pentagon	quadrilaterals	trapezoid	rhombus	parallelograms
decagon	nonagon	octagon	heptagon	hexagon

PYRAMIDS & PRISMS

These three pyramids are located near Gizeh, Egypt.
The true pyramid exists only in Egypt, although other cultures had similar structures.
The largest of these three is called the Great Pyramid of Cheops* and is one of the
Seven Wonders of the World. It is the largest pyramid ever built.

*(2680 B.C.)

pyramid: solid shape with polygon base and triangular sides which meet at one point.

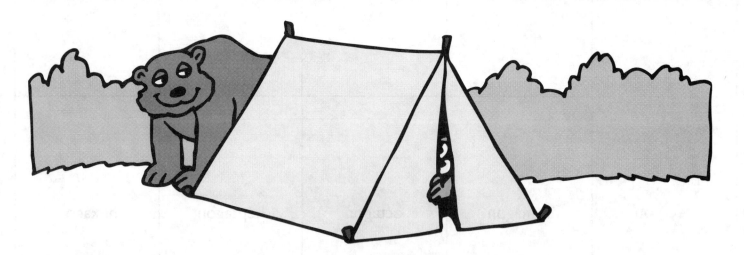

Some tents are triangular prisms. They have two triangular faces, but they do not meet at one point.
(Refer to triangular prism on page 14.)

prism: solid shape with polygon top and base and rectangular sides.

Name _____     **WORKSHEET A**

LEVEL 1, SOLIDS

cube

cylinder

cone

sphere

hemisphere

rectangular solid

Name each solid.

1. _____  4. _____  7. _____

2. _____ 5. _____   8. _____

3. _____ 6. _____   9. _____

10. Give the number of surfaces.

FIGURE	sphere	cube	cylinder	cone	hemisphere	rectangular solid
curved						
flat						

11. On the back, list all the objects you can find or think of that have the shape of one of these six solids. Look around your home, at city buildings, in magazines and in books.

CHALLENGE:
Battle Creek, Michigan, produces more breakfast cereal than any other American city. Which of the six solids named on this page describes a cereal box?

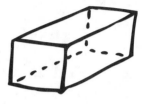

TLC10406 Copyright © Teaching & Learning Company, Carthage, IL 62321-0010

17

Name _____

LEVEL 2, SOLIDS

Give the name of the solid which describes each object.

1. _____

2. _____

3. _____

4. _____

Name these shapes.

5. _____

6. _____

Complete the chart.

FIGURE	7.	8.	9.	10.	11.
Number of Surfaces					
Number of Edges					
Number of Corners					

12. Copy these shapes on isometric dot paper. Then make a figure twice as wide and twice as high.

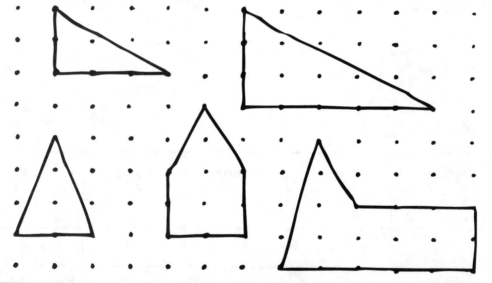

CHALLENGE:
With the discovery of oil in the 1920s, Tulsa, Oklahoma, had more millionaires than any other city in the U.S. This figure is similar to the outline of Oklahoma. Enlarge each side two times on isometric dot paper.

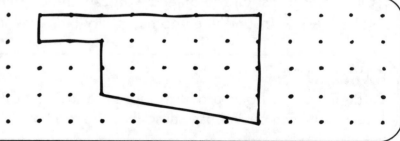

ISOMETRIC DOT PAPER

ISOMETRIC DOT PAPER

LEVEL 3, GEOMETRIC SOLIDS

MATCHING

A.

B.

1. triangular prism _____

2. rectangular prism _____

3. triangular pyramid _____

4. rectangular pyramid_____

C.

D.

5. How many vertices?   A. _____   B. _____   C. _____   D. _____

DEFINE

6. polyhedron:_____

7. cylinder: _____

8. Drawing a Prism

   Step 1: Draw a top. Label the corners.

   Step 2: Draw the base so that it does not overlap with the top. Label the corners.

   Step 3: Connect corresponding corners. Use dotted lines for the edges at the back of the prism.

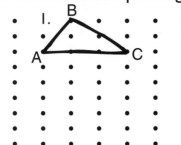

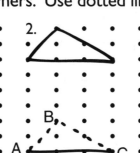

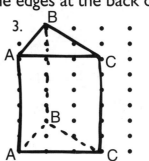

Draw prisms with these bases:

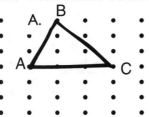

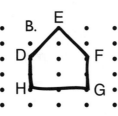

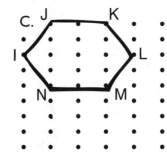

Name _____

LEVEL 4, GEOMETRIC SOLIDS

Identify each solid.

1. _____

2. _____

3. _____

4. _____

5. _____
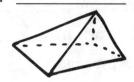

6. _____

7. Complete the chart using the figures above.

FIGURE	1	2	3	4	5	6
flat surfaces						
curved surfaces						
edges						
vertices						

Define each of the following:

8. pyramid: _____

9. prism: _____

If these were folded into a solid, which shapes would they be?

10. _____
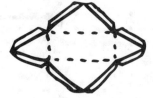

11. _____
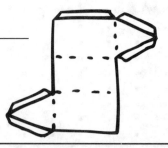

CHALLENGE:
Judith Basin, Montana, has the only sapphire mine in the United States. Draw this model of a faceted sapphire on isometric dot paper with each side twice as long and rotated 1/4 turn to the right.

MATH ART

Pages 23-25 can be used for Level 2 or other levels. Students can cut out figures and decorate for a certain holiday or season. Sides of a solid could picture Valentines, Halloween designs, Hanukkah symbols or winter scenes shown below. Try decorating the cone like an Indian tepee or a Christmas tree. Give each student a copy of the designs for ideas, or cut out designs and glue them on some of the sides before copying them for the students.

After decorating, and cutting out the solids, the students will fold on dotted lines and glue or tape the edges into geometric solids. Using a needle and thread, make a loop through one corner and hang the decorated solid on a Christmas tree or from a thumbtack on a bulletin board.

Students can make a model of a cube with 12 pieces of plastic straws—two inches each—and eight paper clips. Bend paper clips to a 90° angle and spread open as shown on page 29. Make two squares and then attach them with the last four pieces. This helps students count surfaces, edges and corners. This could be decorated with glitter glue for a Christmas ornament or put on a pretty bulletin board.

OCTAHEDRON—8 SIDES

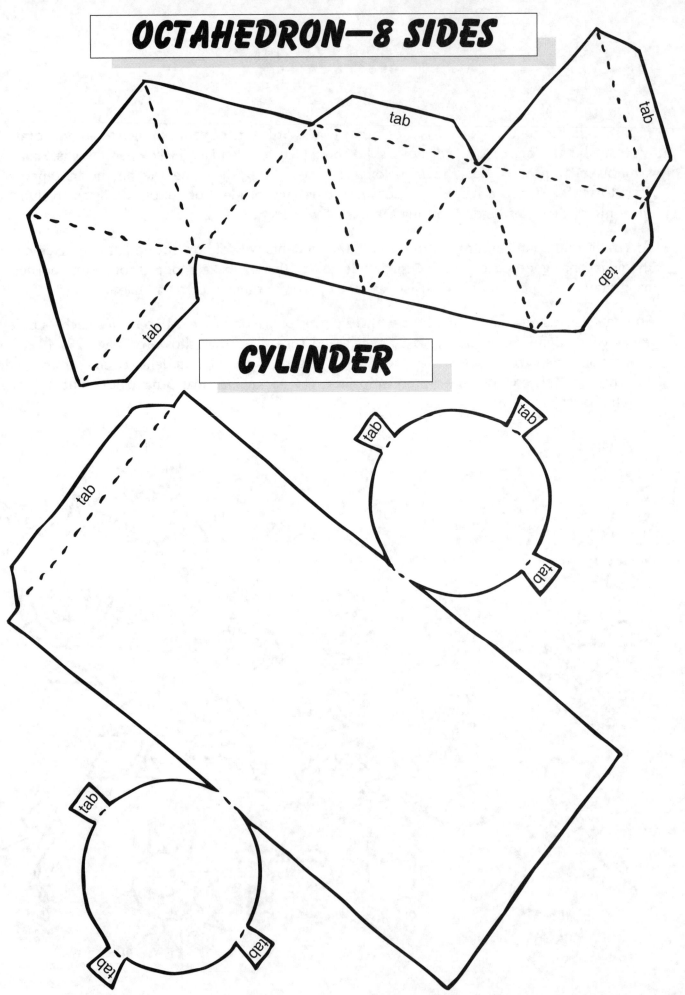

tab

tab

tab

tab

CYLINDER

tab

tab

tab

tab

tab

tab

TRIANGULAR PRISM

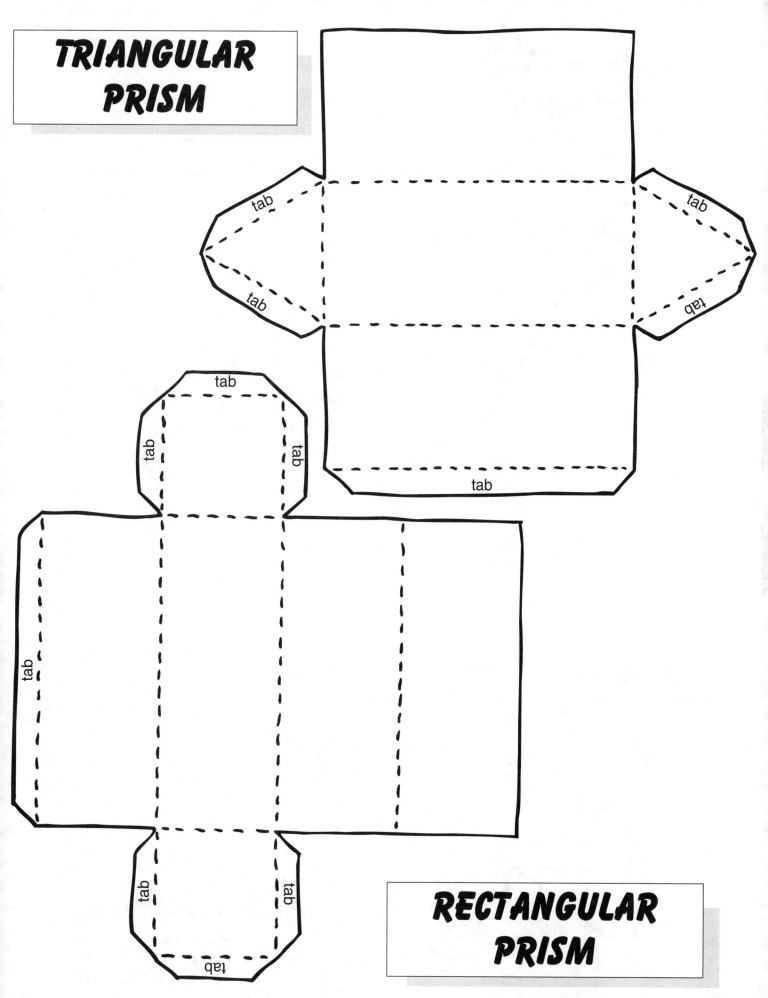

tab

tab

tab

tab

tab

tab

tab

tab

tab

tab

tab

RECTANGULAR PRISM

TRIANGULAR PYRAMID

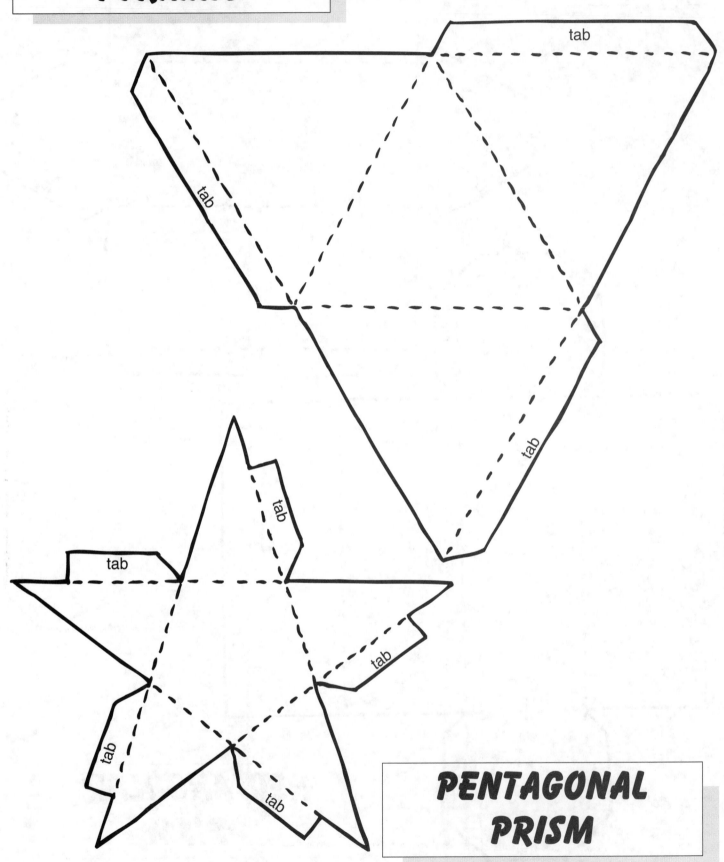

tab

tab

tab

tab

tab

tab

tab

tab

PENTAGONAL PRISM

CUBE

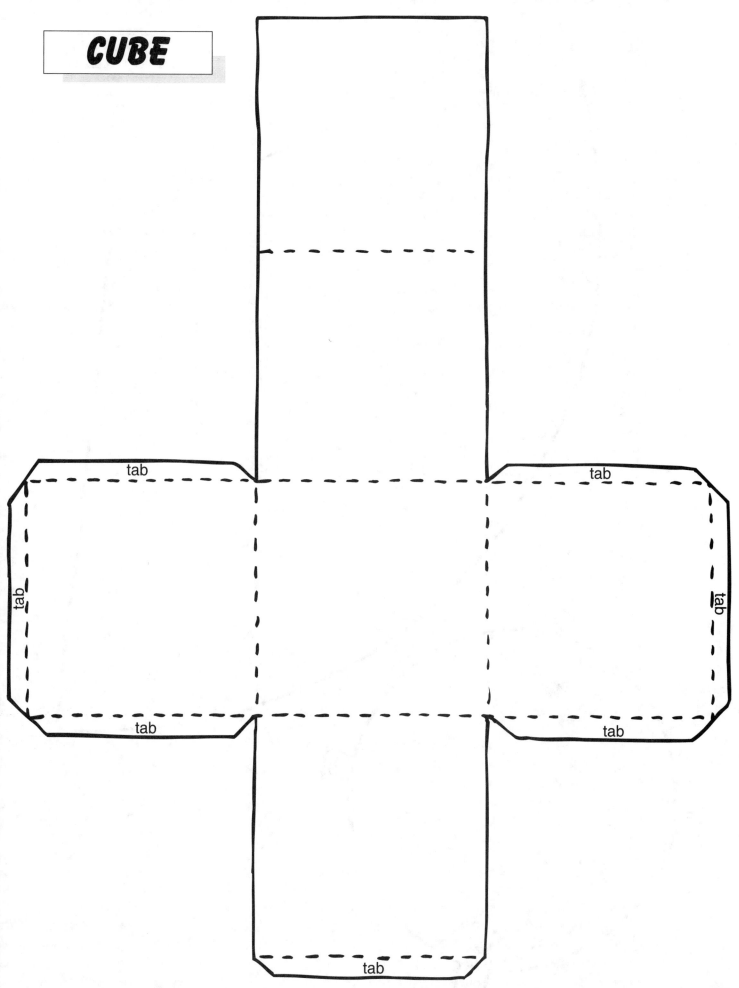

tab

tab

tab

tab

tab

tab

tab

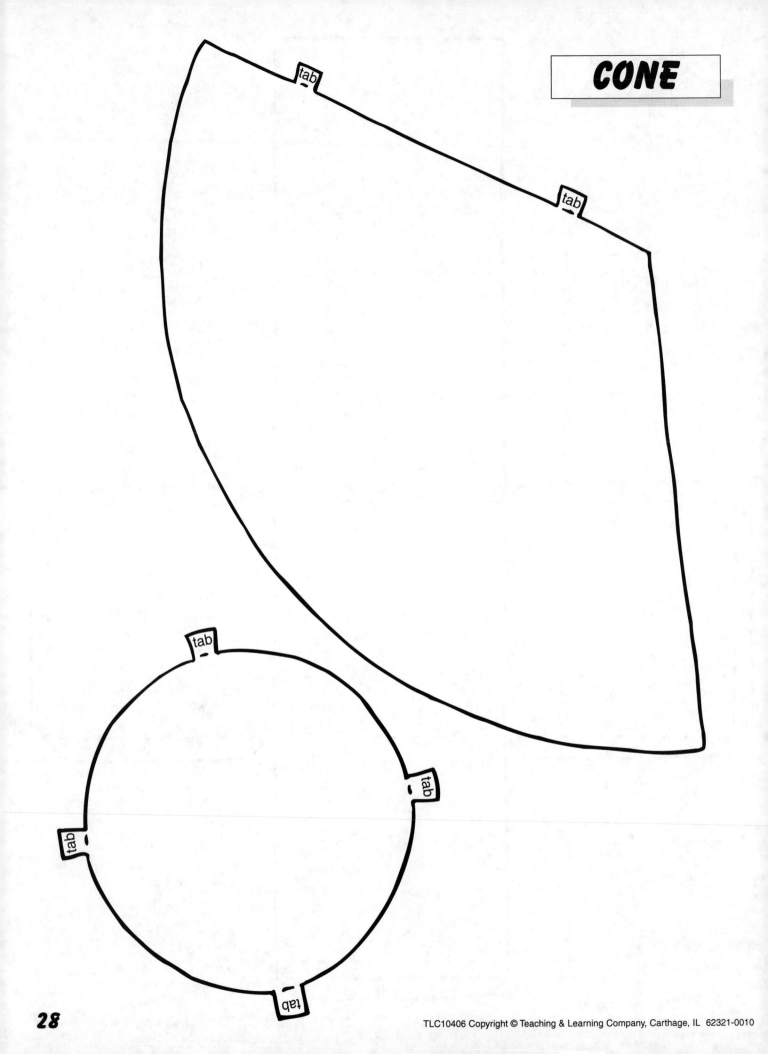

CONE

TRIANGULAR PRISM FROM PLASTIC STRAWS

Materials: 6 1½" pieces plastic straw
3 2" pieces plastic straw
9 small paper clips

Step 1: Cut six pieces of straw 1½" each.
Step 2: Bend six small paper clips to a 60° angle.

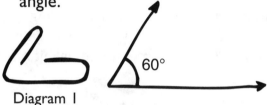

Diagram 1

Step 3: Spread out the loops on each end of each paper clip so the clips will not fall out of the straws.

Diagram 2

Step 4: Form two triangles from the six pieces and the six paper clips.

Diagram 3

Step 5: Press the triangles until the paper clips do not show very much.

Diagram 4

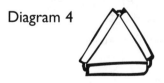

Step 6: Cut three pieces of straw 2" each.
Step 7: Use three more paper clips to attach the 2" pieces between the two triangles.

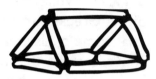

Use this triangular prism to discuss surfaces, edges and vertices of prisms.

OBJECTIVES: For all four levels.

1. Describe, model, enlarge, name and classify plane figures.
2. Relate plane figures to the real world.

MATH HISTORY:
Pythagoras is one of the best-known of the Greeks to study geometry. It is believed that some of his ideas came from the priests of Zoroaster—the wise men or Magi of the Christmas story. They had learned much of their math from the Mesopotamians.

LEVEL 1: Use for third grade or as needed.

1. Introduce four plane figures, polygons and polygon clue words.
2. Relate plane figures to the real world.

CLASSROOM PRESENTATION:
Plane figures have no thickness. Draw these on the board or cut them out of cardboard: square, triangle, rectangle, circle.

These are all closed figures. A nonclosed figure would be:

Characteristics:
square: four equal sides, four equal angles
triangle: three sides, three angles
rectangle: four sides, four equal angles
circle: one curved side, no angles
Polygon: closed plane figure with line segments as sides
Ask students: Which of the four is not a polygon? Circle.

POLYGON CLUE WORDS:

octagon: eight sides—octopus—eight legs
decagon: 10 sides—decade—10 years
quadrilateral: four sides—four
quarters—dollar
trapezoid: trapeze

Use the flash cards on page 14 to illustrate these polygons. Also, the trapezoid muscles let us swing our arms from side to side. Demonstrate the trapezoid muscle.

Students need an understanding of these words for this level worksheet. For Level 2, they will need to memorize definitions.

TAKE-HOME:
Flash cards, pages 12-15, to study plane figures. Worksheet E, page 33; Magic Circles, page 37; Coloring Page, page 39; Isometric Dot Paper, page 19 or 20.

OPTIONAL:
Plane Figures Bingo (page 38) See page 32 for directions.

OPTIONAL:
Math Spelling Test
Spelling words: square, triangle, rectangle, circle, octagon, decagon, trapezoid

LEVEL 2: Use for fourth grade or as needed. Review if needed.

1. Discuss pentagon and parallelogram.
2. Use isometric dot paper to copy and enlarge polygons.

LESSON PLAN 2: PLANE FIGURES

CLASSROOM PRESENTATION:
Discuss parallelogram—four sided polygon with opposite sides parallel.* Discuss the United States Defense Department building—the Pentagon, pictured on page 34.

Review:

polygon: closed plane figure made of line segments

quadrilateral: four-sided polygon

rectangle: four-sided polygon, four equal angles

square: polygon with four equal sides, four equal angles

pentagon: five-sided polygon

octagon: eight-sided polygon

decagon: 10-sided polygon

Demonstrate doubling the length and width of a hexagon:

1. Go down two spaces instead of one.
2. Go over two and up two.
3. Go over two.
4. Go over two and down two.
5. Continue doubling.
6. See page 10 for more directions.

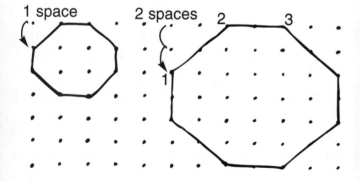

*Squares and rectangles are also parallelograms.

TAKE-HOME:
Flash cards pages 12-15, to study plane figures. Worksheet F, page 34; Magic Circles, page 37; Coloring Page, page 39; Isometric Dot Paper, page 19 or 20.

OPTIONAL:
Plane Figures Bingo (page 38) See page 32 for directions.

LEVEL 3:
Use for fifth grade or as needed. Review if needed.

1. Introduce definitions for geometric terms.
2. Students will draw and double figures.

CLASSROOM PRESENTATION:
Introduce three new terms:

nonagon: nine-sided polygon. *Non* has two Ns as in *nine*.

hexagon: six-sided polygon *Hex* has an X as in *six*.

rhombus: quadrilateral with four equal sides. A rhombus does not have to have equal angles, but it can. A square can be called a rhombus.

DEFINITIONS:
Students must memorize:

polygon: closed plane figure made of line segments

quadrilateral: four-sided polygon

parallelogram: quadrilateral with opposite sides parallel

rectangle: quadrilateral with four equal angles

Use the bingo game to study figures. See the directions on page 32.

TAKE-HOME:
Flash cards pages 12-15, to study plane figures. Worksheet G, page 35; Isometric Dot Paper, page 19 or 20.

OPTIONAL:
Magic Circles, page 37; Coloring Page, page 39.

LEVEL 4: Use for sixth grade or as needed. Review as needed.

1. More definitions.
2. Discuss the term *heptagon*.

CLASSROOM PRESENTATION: Teach these definitions. Refer to other level lesson plans for memory tricks to help students.

polygon: closed plane figure with line segments as sides

quadrilateral: four-sided polygon

parallelogram: four-sided polygon with opposite sides parallel

rhombus: parallelogram with four equal sides

rectangle: quadrilateral with four equal angles

trapezoid: quadrilateral with two opposite sides parallel and two opposite sides not parallel

pentagon: five-sided polygon

hexagon: six-sided polygon

heptagon: seven-sided polygon

octagon: eight-sided polygon

nonagon: nine-sided polygon

decagon: 10-sided polygon

NOTE: In one of the ancient Roman calendars, there were only 10 months. July and August were added later to honor Julius Caesar and Caesar Augustus. For the 10-month calendar, September was the seventh month. Heptagon is seven sided. Hepta and Septe have similar structures.

Use the bingo game to study plane figures, page 38. Mention that there are some plane figures which are not polygons. Put these examples on the board.

C ⊔ (not closed)   ◯ (not a polygon)

TAKE-HOME: Flash cards pages 12-15, to study plane figures. Worksheet H, page 36; Magic Circles instructions, page 37; Coloring Page, page 39.

OPTIONAL: Math Spelling Test
Spelling words: polygon, quadrilateral, parallelogram, rhombus, rectangle, trapezoid, pentagon, hexagon, heptagon, octagon, nonagon, decagon

PLAIN FIGURES BINGO: Copy and laminate bingo cards on page 38 or place each page in a vinyl page protector. Students can cross off squares with crayons or dry-erase markers or small pieces of masking tape. Draw from a pile of plane figures flash cards to call out the names. Show students that many figures can be used in more than one square. A student can only cross off one square for each figure named. These squares have only one correct figure: 10 sides, five sides, nine sides, seven sides, trapezoid, eight sides, three sides, six sides, curved edge. These have more than one correct figure:

any quadrilateral: square, rectangle, parallelogram, rhombus, trapezoid, quadrilateral

four equal angles: square, rectangle

opposite sides parallel: parallelogram, rhombus, square, rectangle

any polygon: any figure except a circle

any plane figure: any figure including a circle

four equal sides: square, rhombus

Name _____

LEVEL 1, PLANE FIGURES

square

triangle

rectangle

circle

MATCHING

_____ 1. one curved side, no angles   a. triangle

_____ 2. three straight sides, three angles   b. circle

_____ 3. four straight sides, four equal angles   c. rectangle

Copy these polygons on isometric dot paper and double each side.

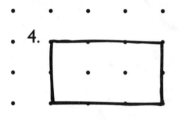

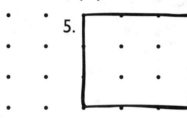

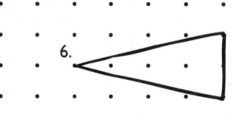

Match the polygon name with the clue word.

_____ 7. quadrilateral   a. octopus

_____ 8. octagon   b. quarter—four in a dollar

_____ 9. decagon   c. trapeze

_____10. trapezoid   d. decade—10 years

REVIEW

_____11. How many surfaces are there on a cube?

_____12. Which solid has one curved and no flat surfaces?

_____13. What is the name of the solid which has the shape of a soup can?

CHALLENGE:

Atlanta, Georgia, has over 40 streets and roads with the name "Peachtree" in their names. Look at the state flag of Georgia. List all the plane figures in the flag. How many of each can you find?

Name _____

LEVEL 2, PLANE FIGURES

MATCHING

____ 1. decagon
____ 2. square
____ 3. pentagon
____ 4. triangle
____ 5. octagon

a. three sides
b. eight sides
c. 10 sides
d. four sides
e. five sides

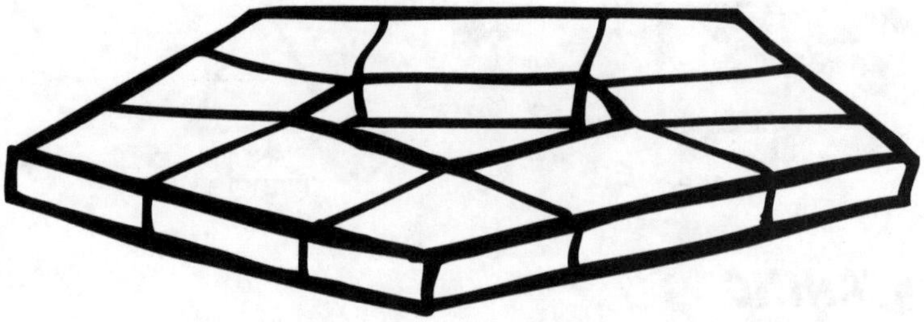

U.S. Department of Defense—The Pentagon

Draw these on isometric dot paper. Then double each side.

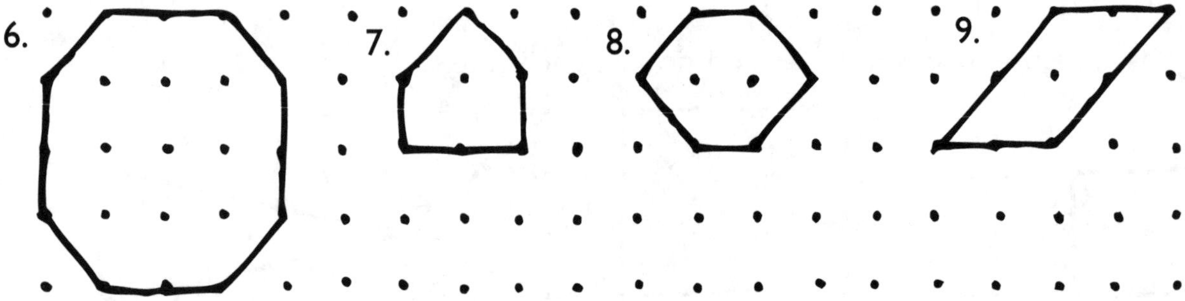

6.   7.   8.   9.

Write down the letters of each. (There will be more than one right answer for some.)

____10. polygons: closed plane figures made of line segments

____11. quadrilaterals: polygons having four sides

____12. parallelograms: four-sided polygons with opposite sides parallel

____13. rectangles: four-sided polygon, four right angles

a.    d.

b.   e.

c.    f.

REVIEW

____14. How many edges on a cube?

____15. How many corners on a rectangular solid?

CHALLENGE:

Oregon is one of our nation's leaders in producing lumber for homes and furniture. One furniture store calls this end table "the pyramid." Why?
_____ What other name could they use? _____
Which one is better? _____

34

TLC10406 Copyright © Teaching & Learning Company, Carthage, IL 62321-0010

LEVEL 3, QUADRILATERAL

DEFINE

1. polygon: _____

2. quadrilateral: _____

3. parallelogram: _____

4. rectangle: _____

MATCHING

_____ 5. nonagon   a. six-sided polygon

_____ 6. pentagon   b. polygon, four equal sides

_____ 7. hexagon   c. nine-sided polygon

_____ 8. rhombus   d. five-sided polygon

9. Draw a decagon on isometric dot paper and double the size.

10. Draw a parallelogram on isometric dot paper and double the size.

MATCHING   Some have more than one answer.

_____ 11. polygons

_____ 12. quadrilaterals

_____ 13. parallelograms

_____ 14. rectangles

_____ 15. squares

a.

b.

c.

d.

e.

REVIEW

_____ 16. How many vertices on a cube?

_____ 17. Which solid has rectangular sides and triangle top and base? _____

CHALLENGE:

New York state is a national leader in book publishing and toy manufac-turing. This 3 x 3 x 3 cube is colored on all six sides. How many of the small cubes are colored on: _____ three sides   _____ two sides
_____ one sides   _____ zero sides

LEVEL 4, PLANE FIGURES

DEFINE

1. polygon: _____

2. quadrilateral: _____

3. rhombus: _____

4. hexagon: _____

5. nonagon: _____

6. octagon: _____

7. heptagon: _____

8. pentagon: _____

9. decagon: _____

MATCHING

____10. parallelogram   a. parallel with four equal angles

____11. rectangle   b. quadrilateral with two sides parallel and two not parallel

____12. trapezoid   c. quadrilateral with opposite sides parallel

REVIEW

____13. Which plane figure is not a polygon?

____14. Which solid has exactly one curved surface and no flat surface?

____15. Which government building in Washington, D.C., is named after a polygon?

____16. Which solid has polygon base and triangular sides which meet at one point?

____17. Which solid has polygon top and base and rectangular sides?

CHALLENGE:

The state of Maryland is known for two important firsts: first in the colonies to offer freedom of religion in 1634 and first to sell ice cream commercially in 1851! What are the two geometric solids which form this ice cream treat? _____, _____

MAGIC CIRCLES

This is a "magic trick" that you can use to puzzle an adult or friend.

Directions
1. Cut out the "magic circles" card.
2. Ask someone to pick a number in one of the circles and point to all the circles that contain that number.
3. The number for each circle is shown on the page. Memorize the numbers of each circle, 1, 2, 3 or 4.
4. Add the numbers of the circles the person has pointed to. If they point to all 4, add 4 + 3 + 2 + 1 = 10. The number they picked is 10. If they point to 4, 2 and 1, the number is 7.

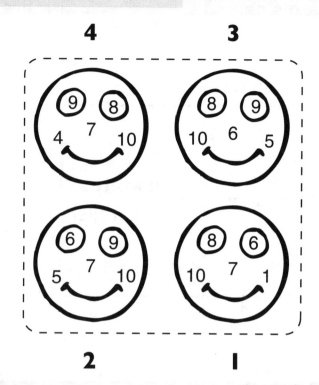

ACTIVITY PAGE

MAGIC CIRCLES

This is a "magic trick" that you can use to puzzle an adult or friend.

Directions
1. Cut out the "magic circles" card.
2. Ask someone to pick a number in one of the circles and point to all the circles that contain that number.
3. The number for each circle is shown on the page. Memorize the numbers of each circle, 1, 2, 3 or 4.
4. Add the numbers of the circles the person has pointed to. If they point to all 4, add 4 + 3 + 2 + 1 = 10. The number they picked is 10. If they point to 4, 2 and 1, the number is 7.

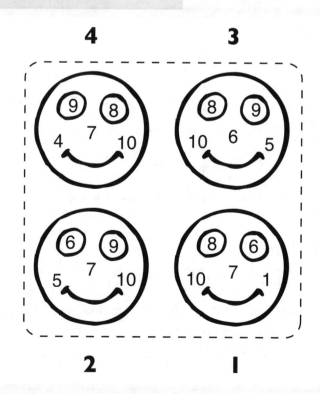

ten sides	any quadrilateral	five sides	four equal angles	nine sides
seven sides	opposite sides parallel	trapezoid	any polygon	any plane figure
eight sides	four equal angles	**FREE**	three sides	six sides
any plane figure	six sides	ten sides	opposite sides parallel	five sides
four equal sides	curved side figure	seven sides	any quadrilateral	eight sides

Name _____

Choose four colors: color 1 _____—squares with a dot; color 2 _____—squares with no dot;
color 3 _____—pentagons with a dot; color 4 _____—pentagons without a dot.

LESSON PLAN 3: POINTS, LINES, PLANES & ANGLES

OBJECTIVES: For all four levels.

1. Understand basic components of geometry—point, line, plane, segment, ray and angle.
2. Develop the process of measuring angles.
3. Learn terms for classifying angles.

MATH HISTORY: Rene Descartes was only 20 years old when he began developing his new way of teaching geometry. His ideas regarding logical thinking were so brilliant that they carried over into all fields of learning. He was first to devise the idea of using graph paper to locate points and design lines and curves.

LEVEL 1: Use for third grade or as needed.

1. Introduce line segments and their endpoints.
2. Discuss naming segments, segments in a plane figure and intersection of two segments.

CLASSROOM PRESENTATION: One section of a straight line with two endpoints is called a line segment. If it is curved, it is not a segment.

(not a segment)

(segments)

A line segment (or simply segment) is named by its endpoints.

A •————————• B

This is written $\overline{AB}$ or $\overline{BA}$ and read segment AB or segment BA.

The point where two segments cross is called the intersection of the two segments. Students should think of the intersection of two streets.

Intersection

Review the number of sides in a quadrilateral, pentagon, hexagon, heptagon, octagon, nonagon and decagon. These sides are also line segments.

TAKE-HOME: Worksheet I, page 43; Coloring Page, page 48.

OPTIONAL: Plane Figures Bingo (pages 38) to reinforce knowing those terms.

LEVEL 2: Lines, Rays & Angles: Use for fourth grade or as needed.

1. Introduce lines, rays and angles.
2. Discuss naming lines, rays and angles.

LESSON PLAN 3: POINTS, LINES, PLANES & ANGLES

CLASSROOM PRESENTATION: If a segment is extended past both endpoints and does not end, it is a line. Ask students to name things in our world which are like lines. Example: telephone wires, stripe down a road. These always have an end, so they are not exactly like a "line" in geometry. When we say line we mean a straight line, not a curved one. Lines are named by using two points on the line and are drawn with an arrow on each end:

This is written $\overleftrightarrow{CD}$ or $\overleftrightarrow{DC}$ and read line CD or line DC.

A ray has one endpoint and extends in one direction without ending. Ask students if they can think of examples: beam of a flashlight, jet trail.

This is written $\overrightarrow{EF}$ and read ray EF. Ray FE would be: The two are not the same.

An angle is formed by two rays having the same endpoint. This is named ABC or CBA. It is also called angle B. B is the vertex of the angle.

When an angle forms a square corner, it is called a right angle. The little box inside the angle means right angle.

This angle is smaller than a right angle:

This angle is larger than a right angle:

Angles are always made up of rays, not line segments.

(not an angle)

TAKE-HOME: Worksheet J, page 44; Coloring Page, page 48.

OPTIONAL: Math Spelling Test
Spelling words: point, segment, line, angle, ray, intersection

LEVEL 3: Use for fifth grade or as needed.
1. Introduce a right-oriented protractor.
2. Discuss the degrees marked on a protractor.
3. Define *acute* and *obtuse* angles.

CLASSROOM PRESENTATION: Show the students a right-oriented protractor. This means the 0 is located at the right side of the protractor. If you do not have a large wooden classroom protractor, use the one on page 47. Enlarge, copy on cardstock, laminate and use it at your chalkboard. It could also be used with an overhead projector.

In the human body, the protractor muscle lets you extend an arm or leg. You can form an angle with your elbow as the vertex of the angle. The angle can be a right angle, larger or smaller. (Demonstrate with your own arm.)

right angle — acute angle — obtuse angle

The "square corner" angle has 90°. (Demonstrate on the protractor.) An angle with a measure less than 90° is called an acute angle. If an angle has more than 90° in its measure, it is an obtuse angle.

CLUE WORD:

To remember what an acute angle is, think of a "cute" *little* angle—smaller than 90°.

TAKE-HOME:
Worksheet K, page 45; Coloring Page, page 48.

OPTIONAL:
Math Spelling Test
Spelling words: point, segment, line, angle, ray, intersection, acute, obtuse

TAKE-HOME:
Give each student a copy of the large protractor, page 47, a vinyl page protector and a crayon or dry-erase marker. Have each row of students draw an angle on the page protector. The black dot at the center of the protractor is the vertex of the angle. For a 30° angle, draw one ray through the 0 and the other through the 30. Example: row 1 draws 30°, row two draws 70°, row 3 draws 110°. Have students check each other. Students erase the angles with a tissue. Now give them 45°, 85°, 125°, for example. Then 62°, 87°, etc.

LEVEL 4:
Use for sixth grade or as needed. Review if needed.

1. Discuss 360 degrees in a circle and drawing angles.
2. Introduce perpendicular lines and planes.

CLASSROOM PRESENTATION:
Show the 360° protractor on the worksheet, page 46. Measuring the degrees in an angle has many applications from architectural designs to navigation at sea and in the air. How many degrees in the angle on the worksheet? 35°

The 360° circle has been used for many centuries and will be discussed again in Lesson Plan 7. See page 78 for more information on the 360° circle.

If two lines intersect and form four right angles, the lines are said to be perpendicular.

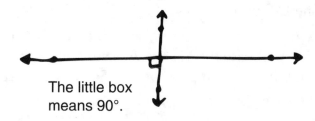

The little box means 90°.

A plane is a flat surface extending in all directions without ending. Think of a tabletop that extends in all directions. To name a plane, name any three points in the plane and not all in the same line. Use four students, three pencils and a hardback book. Have the three students hold the pencil points even and the fourth place the book on the three points. The three pencil points control the plane that the cover of the book touches. If one pencil moves, the position of the plane moves.

TAKE-HOME:
Worksheet L, page 46; Activity Page, page 47; Coloring Page, page 48.

OPTIONAL:
Math Spelling Test
Spelling words: point, segment, line, angle, ray, intersection, acute, obtuse, perpendicular, degrees, protractor

Name _____

1. Circle the line segments.

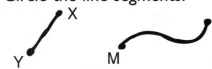

2. What are the two names for this segment? A •————• B

_____ _____   Name the endpoints. _____

3. Name the segments that form this triangle. _____

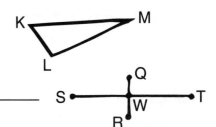

_____ _____

4. Name the point at which these two segments intersect. _____

5. How many line segments in each shape?

a. _____   b. _____   c. _____   d. _____

      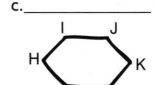   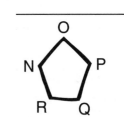

REVIEW

6. Name each solid.

a. _____   b. _____   c. _____   d. _____

7. Name each plane figure.

a. _____   b. _____   c. _____   d. _____

MATCHING

8. _____ decagon   a. four sides

   _____ octagon   b. eight sides

   _____ quadrilateral   c. 10 sides

CHALLENGE:
The lowest "point" in the Western Hemisphere is located at Death Valley in California, 282 feet below sea level. How many line segments are there in the outline of the map of California?

Name _____

LEVEL 2, LINES, RAYS & ANGLES

1. Name the two rays. _____ _____

2. Give three names for this angle. _____ _____ _____

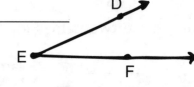

3. Name these two lines. _____ _____

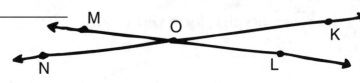

Name all the angles _____ _____ _____ _____

4. Name the right angle. _____
   Name the angle larger than the right angle. _____
   Name the angle smaller than the right angle. _____

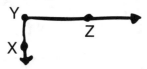  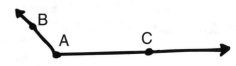

5. Draw a right angle. Label the three points. Be sure it has two rays.

REVIEW

6. How many sides? a. _____ quadrilateral   b. _____ triangle   c. _____ octagon   d. _____ decagon
   e. _____ pentagon   f. _____ square

MATCHING

7. _____pyramid   a.   b.
   _____prism

CHALLENGE:

North Dakota is the home of the Theodore Roosevelt National Park preserve—a sanctuary for buffalo, wild horses, mule deer, pronghorn antelope, bighorn sheep and prairie dogs. It has a higher percentage of farmers than any other state. Which geometric solid is the same shape as this bale of hay?

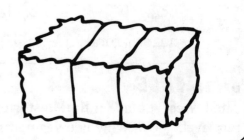

LEVEL 3, ACUTE, OBTUSE & RIGHT ANGLES

1. Name the right angle. _____

2. Name the acute angle. _____

3. Name the obtuse angle. _____

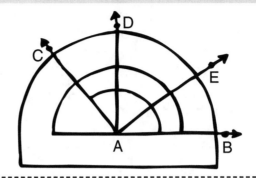

---

4. Name the acute angles. _____ _____ _____

   Name the obtuse angles. _____ _____ _____

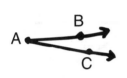 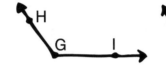 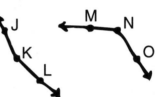 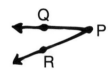

---

5. Label the rays correctly.

   right angle = ∠BOC

   20° angle = ∠COA

   50° angle = ∠COD

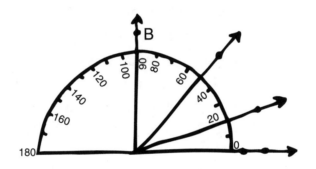

REVIEW/MATCHING

_____ 6. trapezoid   a. solid, polygon base, triangular sides meet at one point

_____ 7. parallelogram   b. quadrilateral, four right angles

_____ 8. rectangle   c. quadrilateral, two sides parallel, two sides not

_____ 9. pentagon   d. polygon top and base, sides are rectangles

_____ 10. hexagon   e. quadrilateral, opposite sides parallel

_____ 11. prism   f. five-sided polygon

_____ 12. pyramid   g. six-sided polygon

CHALLENGE:
Texas has the tallest monument in all 50 states. The San Jacinto monument is 15 feet taller than the Washington Monument. On the flag of Texas, mark one acute angle and one right angle. Label them ∠A and ∠R. How many rectangles can you find in this flag? _____ How many squares? _____

LEVEL 4, ANGLES, PLANES & PERPENDICULAR LINES

1. Label each angle as acute or obtuse.

a. _____   b. _____   c. _____

d. _____   e. _____   f. _____

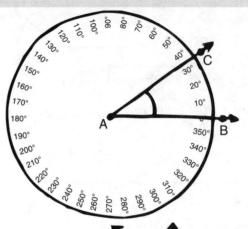

2. Name the pair of perpendicular lines. _____ _____

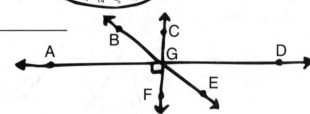

MATCHING

_____ 3. acute angle
_____ 4. perpendicular lines
_____ 5. segment
_____ 6. obtuse
_____ 7. ray
_____ 8. protractor

a. part of a line with two endpoints
b. more than 90°
c. less than 90°
d. two lines forming four right angles
e. used to draw and measure angles
f. part of a line that has one endpoint and extends in the other direction

9. Draw angles of 50°, 90°, 125°.

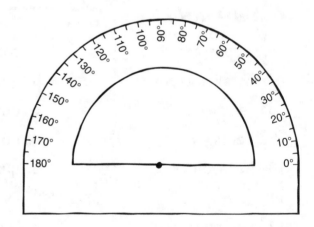

10. How many degrees in a complete circle? _____

REVIEW

11. How many sides? a. _____ octagon   b. _____ pentagon   c. _____ hexagon   d. _____ nonagon
    e. _____ quadrilateral

CHALLENGE:
Utah's nickname is the Beehive State. Find a picture of a honeycomb. What shape are the cells of a honeycomb?

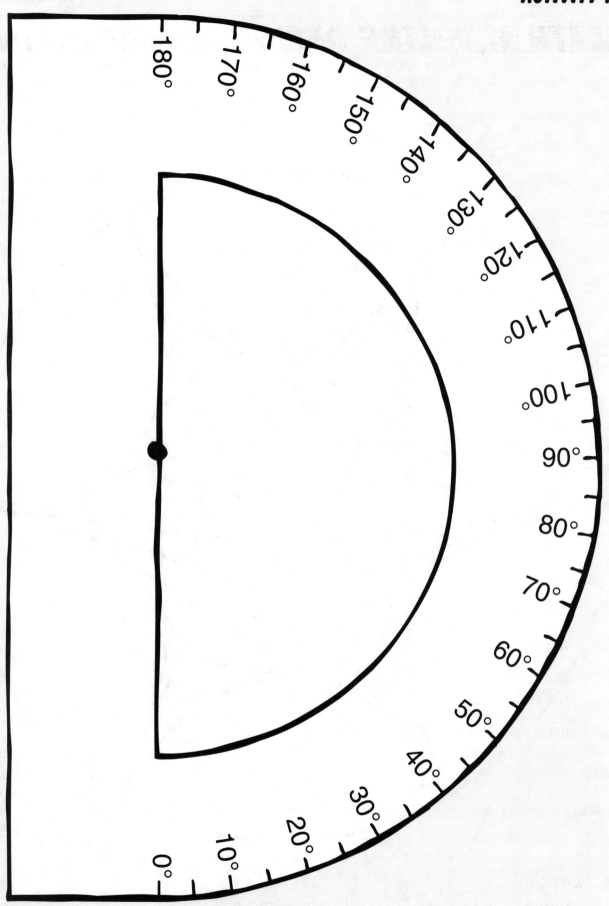

MATH ART—LINE DESIGN, CURVES MADE OF LINES!

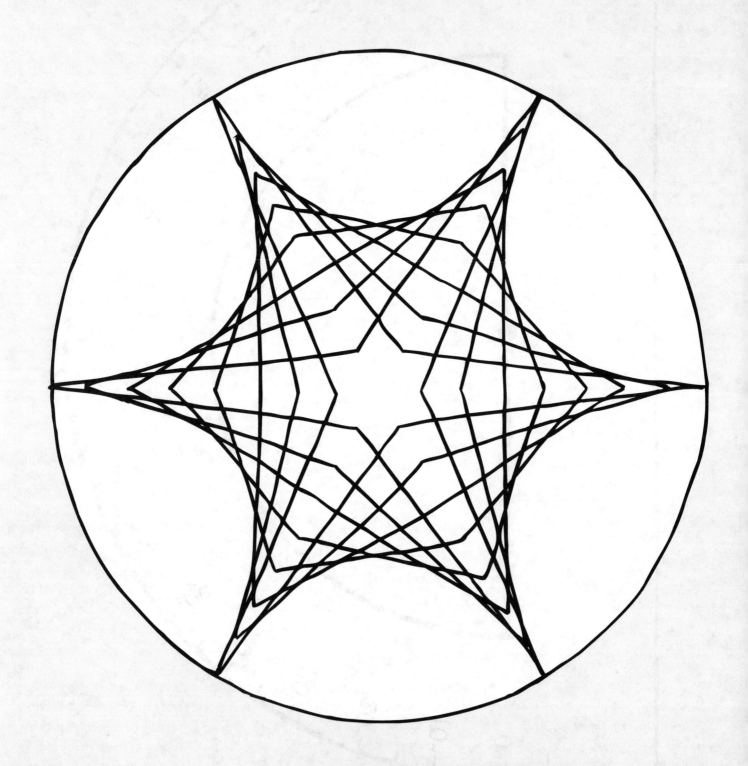

LESSON PLAN 4: METRIC SYSTEM

OBJECTIVES: For all four levels.

1. Understand the structure of the metric system for measuring lengths of objects.
2. Understand the approximate length of millimeters, centimeters, decimeters, meters and kilometers.
3. Learn clue words to help in remembering unit names.
4. Measure some objects using metric units.

(Note: Post the wall charts, pages 54-55, and leave them up. Give copies to each student for their notebooks. Seeing something repeatedly is a great memory aid.)

MATH HISTORY: The length of a meter was originally intended to be $1/10,000,000$ of the distance from the equator to either pole. Remember the meaning of the word *geometry*? ..."Earth measure!" They truly measured the Earth to determine the length of the meter. However, someone made a mistake in measurement! The meter is now the distance between two scratches on a metal bar at Sevres, France, near Paris, not $1/10,000,000$ of the equator to pole distance.

LEVEL 1: Use for third grade or as needed.

1. Display objects which are about one centimeter, one decimeter and one meter.
2. Discuss abbreviations for metric units: cm, dm and mm.
3. Change from cm to m and from m to cm.
4. Measure students' heights in decimeters and centimeters.

CLASSROOM PRESENTATION: Bring two soup cans to the classroom. Soup cans are almost exactly one decimeter in height. Cut out the labels, page 53, and attach to the cans. Leave these in the classroom while teaching metrics. Discuss the decimeter with the students. If possible, stack up 10 cans so students will have a mental image of one meter.

Give each student or group of students page 7 for making a decimeter stick and a millimeter stick.

Discuss the wall chart on page 54. Show students one meter related to the distance from the doorknob to the floor. Stack the 10 soup cans up next to the doorknob. Also show that a yardstick is about 1 meter long.

Show students the soup can that says 10 cm = 1 dm. If 10 soup cans = 1 meter, how many centimeters in 1 meter? (100) How many in 2 meters? (200) If you have 300 cm, how many meters do you have? (3) Put on the board:

  1 m = 100 cm   7 cm = 700 cm

To change from meters to centimeters, add two zeros.

  500 cm = 5 m   400 cm = _____ m

To change from centimeters to meters, remove two zeros.

Bring a craft stick to the classroom. The width is about one centimeter. Discuss whether objects are more or less than a meter in length.

Examples: football field, fingernail file, hammer, house, etc.

The abbreviation for *meter* is m and for *centimeter* is cm.

TAKE-HOME: Worksheet M, page 57. Have each student cut off the centimeter ruler at the right side of the worksheet. Have each one practice measuring one or two objects (examples: math book, chalkboard eraser, pencil eraser, etc.), and have students check each other to see if they are right.

OPTIONAL: Identification Cards, page 56. Copy this page on cardstock. Have a parent or classroom aid help measure each student with a decimeter stick. Add a zero to find centimeters. If the student is exactly halfway between two decimeter marks, round to the larger number. Laminate the cards.

LESSON PLAN 4: METRIC SYSTEM

LEVEL 2: Use for fourth grade or as needed.

1. Continue discussion of decimeters and centimeters.
2. Practice changing from one unit to another.
3. Learn to change from inches to decimeters.
4. Learn clue words.

CLASSROOM PRESENTATION: Review Level 1. Teach clue words at the top of Worksheet N, page 58. Use these unit values to change from one unit to another:

1 m = 10 dm	1 dm = .1 m
1 m = 100 cm	1 cm = .01 m

Do some sample problems:

4 m = _____ dm—Multiply 4 x 10

6 m = _____ cm—Multiply 6 x 100

8 dm = _____ m—Multiply by .1

2 cm = _____ m—Multiply by .01

A decimeter is about four inches. If a book is about 12 inches long, how many decimeters? Divide by 4. (3 dm) Draw a 12-inch line on the board. Measure with the decimeter stick. Have groups of students take turns measuring the classroom in meters, dm and cm.

TAKE-HOME: Worksheet N, page 58.

OPTIONAL: Have one group of students measure the classroom while others watch. All students mark the measurements on their worksheets. Identification Cards, page 56.

LEVEL 3: Use for fifth grade or as needed. Review Levels 1 and 2.

1. Discuss clue word for *millimeter*.
2. Discuss using millimeters to measure lengths.

CLASSROOM PRESENTATION: Review the wall charts on pages 54-55. (Doorknob to floor, craft stick, pencil lead.) Clue words for dm and cm? (Decade and century.) How many?

1 m = _____ dm   1 m = _____ cm

New clue words: *Millennium* is 1000 years. One meter is 1000 millimeters.

NOTE: When a metric unit is less than one meter, the name has an l just before the *meter* part of the word.

DEC<u>I</u>METER   CENT<u>I</u>METER   MILL<u>I</u>METER

In Level 4, students will start to learn the labels larger than one meter—kilometer first.

TAKE-HOME: Worksheet O, page 59; Wall Charts, pages 54-55.

OPTIONAL: Discuss which objects would be measured in meters, centimeters or millimeters: width of the tip on a ball-point pen, (mm), textbook (cm or mm), parking lot (m), etc.

LEVEL 4: Use for sixth grade or as needed. Review Levels 1-3.

1. Introduce kilometer measurements.
2. Illustrate changing inches to centimeters and meters to inches.
3. Reinforce all that was learned in earlier levels.

CLASSROOM PRESENTATION:

1 kilometer = 1000 meters. Abbreviation for *kilometer* is km or sometimes just k. How long is a 5 k race? 5000 meters.

How long is each of these in meters:

10 dm = 1 meter	1 km = 1000 m
1 cm = .01 m	1 mm = .001 m

Remind students that when the letter l is in the middle of the metric label, the unit is less than one meter. Then they recall the clue words:

decade = 10 years
century = 100 years
millennium = 1000 years

1 meter = 10 decimeters
1 meter = 100 centimeters
1 meter = 1000 millimeters

Remind students about the height of the doorknob above the floor; remind them of the width of the craft stick; remind them of the height of the soup can. Point out the soup can with the decimeter label. Use the wall chart on page 54. They need a concept of each of these units.

If students have a centimeter ruler, ask them to see about how many centimeters there are in one inch. There are about 2.5. Draw a 10-inch line on the board. Ask how to find the number of centimeters in 10 inches. 10 inches = _____ cm. If there are 2.5 in one inch, multiply 10 inches times 2.5. (The answer is 10 inches x 2.5 = 25 cm.)

There are about 39.4 inches in one meter. If a room is 10 meters long, how many inches long is it? 10 x 39.4 = 394 inches.

TAKE-HOME: Worksheet P, page 60.

OPTIONAL: Metric Unit Guide, page 52. Although the worksheets in this book do not include problems about decameters (pronounced DECK-A-METERS) or hectometers, page 52 has a brief guide for changing from one unit to another. You may copy this for students to keep in their math notebooks until they do study these units.

METRIC UNIT GUIDE

1 kilometer (km) = 1000 meters

1 hectometer (hm) = 100 meters

1 decameter (dam) = 10 meters

1 meter (m) = 1 meter

1 decimeter (dm) = .1 meter

1 centimeter (cm) = .01 meter

1 millimeter (mm) = .001 meter

(All the units with the letter 1 just before the word *meter* are less than one meter.)

1. To change from one unit to another, first think which unit is larger and which one is smaller.

2. To change from a larger unit to a smaller unit, multiply by 10 or a power of 10. You can also think of moving the decimal to the right. Use this chart:

$$\begin{array}{ccccccc} \text{x10} & \text{x10} & \text{x10} & \text{x10} & \text{x10} & \text{x10} \\ \text{km} & \text{hm} & \text{dam} & \text{m} & \text{dm} & \text{cm} & \text{mm} \end{array}$$

To change from centimeters to millimeters, you are going from a larger unit to a smaller unit—you must multiply. You are moving one space on the chart—multiply by 10.

13 cm = 130 mm

To change from hectometers to decimeters, you are going from a larger unit to a smaller unit—you must multiply. You are moving three spaces on the chart—multiply by 10 x 10 x 10 or 1000—or move the decimal three places.

25 hm = 25,000 dm
(25,<u>000</u>)

3. To change from a smaller unit to a larger unit, divide by 10 or a power of 10. You can also think of moving the decimal to the left. Use this chart:

$$\begin{array}{ccccccc} \text{km} & \text{hm} & \text{dam} & \text{m} & \text{dm} & \text{cm} & \text{mm} \\ \div 10 & \div 10 & \div 10 & \div 10 & \div 10 & \div 10 \end{array}$$

To change from decimeters to meters, divide by 10.

15 dm = 1.5 m

To change from centimeters to hectometers, you are moving four spaces on the chart. Divide by 10 x 10 x 10 x 10 or move the decimal four places to the left.

3000 cm = .3 hm
(<u>3000</u>)

TLC10406 Copyright © Teaching & Learning Company, Carthage, IL 62321-0010

SOUP CAN LABELS

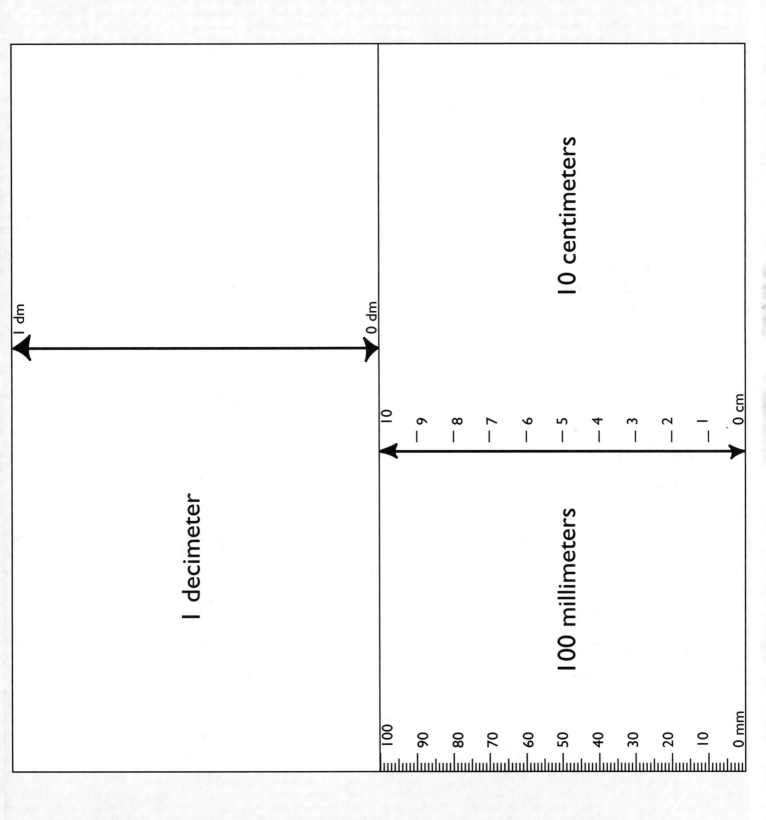

1 decimeter

1 dm

0 dm

10 centimeters

10 9 8 7 6 5 4 3 2 1 0 cm

100 millimeters

100 90 80 70 60 50 40 30 20 10 0 mm

METRIC CLUE WORDS

1 METER
About the distance from a doorknob to the floor. (Also about 1 yard.)

1 METER

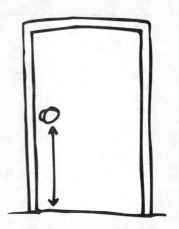

1 DECIMETER
About the height of a soup can.

1 DECIMETER

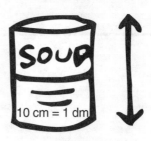

10 cm = 1 dm

1 CENTIMETER
About the width of a craft stick.

1 CENTIMETER

1 MILLIMETER
About the width of a pencil lead.

1 MILLIMETER

NOTE: For units less than a meter, there is always a letter l just before the word *meter*.

TLC10406 Copyright © Teaching & Learning Company, Carthage, IL 62321-0010

METRIC UNITS OF MEASURE

KEEP THESE SIMILARITIES IN MIND . . .

Kilometers are used like miles.

Meters are used like yards.

Centimeters are used like inches.

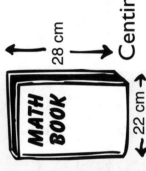

28 cm
22 cm

1 KILOMETER (KM) = 1000 METERS
1 HECTOMETER (HM) = 100 METERS
1 DECAMETER (DAM) = 10 METERS
1 METER (M)
1 DECIMETER (DM) = .1 METER
1 CENTIMETER (CM) = .01 METER
1 MILLIMETER (MM) = .001 METER

REMEMBER . . .

When a metric label has the letter l right before the word meter, it is less than one meter.

Name _____

Address _____

Height: _____ cm _____ dm

Name _____

Address _____

Height: _____ cm _____ dm

Name _____

Address _____

Height: _____ cm _____ dm

Name _____

Address _____

Height: _____ cm _____ dm

Name _____

Address _____

Height: _____ cm _____ dm

Name _____

Address _____

Height: _____ cm _____ dm

Name _____

Address _____

Height: _____ cm _____ dm

Name _____

Address _____

Height: _____ cm _____ dm

Name _____

Address _____

Height: _____ cm _____ dm

IDENTIFICATION CARDS

Name _____   **WORKSHEET M**

LEVEL 1, METRIC SYSTEM

MATCHING

_____ 1. one centimeter is about   a. the distance from a doorknob to the floor

_____ 2. one meter is about   b. the width of a craft stick

3. Fill in the blanks.   Remember . . . 1 meter = 100 centimeters   100 cm = 1 m

a. 2 m = 200 cm   e. 300 cm = _____ m

b. 5 m = _____ cm   f. 400 cm = _____ m

c. 9 m = _____ cm   g. 700 cm = _____ m

d. 10 m = _____ cm   h. 800 cm = _____ m

4. Is it more than a meter? Write *yes* or *no*.

_____ a. length of a bus   _____ c. length of a football field

_____ b. length of a pencil   _____ d. length of a hammer

5. Cut off the centimeter ruler at the right. Find three things shorter than 26 centimeters. Write the names of the objects and their lengths. Round off to the nearest centimeter. If it is exactly halfway, round to the larger number.

Object	Length
_____	_____ cm
_____	_____ cm
_____	_____ cm

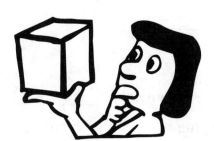

REVIEW

6. How many sides are there on a cube? _____

7. Which plane figure is not a polygon? _____

8. Name this segment. _____   B •————————• A

CHALLENGE:

Alaska has more tidewater glaciers than any other spot in the world. Would it be easier to measure a glacier in meters or centimeters? _____

Ruler markings: 1 2 3 4 5 6 7 8 9 10 11 12 13 14 15 16 17 18 19 20 21 22 23 24 25 26

LEVEL 2, METRIC SYSTEM

Clue Words

A year is $^1/10$ of a decade. A *decimeter* is $^1/10$ of a meter. A dollar is 100 cents. A *meter* is 100 centimeters.

Fill in the blanks.

1. A meter is about the distance from a _____ to the floor.

2. A centimeter is about the width of a _____.

3. A decimeter is about the height of a _____.

4. 5 m = _____ cm

5. 3 m = _____ dm

6. 9 m = _____ cm

7. 3 dm = _____ m

8. 7 cm = _____ m

9. 2 m = _____ dm

Remember

1 m = 10 dm	1 dm = .1 m
1 m = 100 cm	1 cm = .01 m

10. A decimeter is about 4 inches. If a table is 48 inches wide, how wide would it be in decimeters? _____

11. Find your height in inches. _____ Change to decimeters. _____

12. What is the length of your classroom in meters? _____ In decimeters? _____ In centimeters? _____

REVIEW

13. Is this angle a right angle? _____

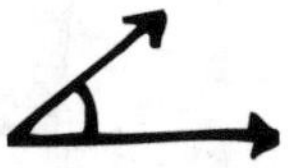

14. Name the segment. _____ Name the ray. _____   O   N

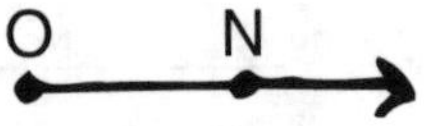

15. What is the name of the solid that is the shape of a soup can? _____

16. Name the five-sided plane figure. _____

17. Name the 10-sided plane figure. _____

CHALLENGE:

Carthage, Illinois, is the home of the Teaching & Learning Company, publisher of the Math Phonics™ books. If a Math Phonics™ book measures 2.2 decimeters by 2.8 decimeters, what is the size in centimeters? _____ In meters? _____

LEVEL 3, METRIC SYSTEM

Clue Words

1000 years is a millennium. 1000 millimeters is a meter.

1. Fill in the blanks.

   a. 1 meter = _____ decimeters

   b. 1 decimeter = _____ meters

   c. 1 meter = _____ centimeters

   d. 1 centimeter = _____ meters

   e. 1 meter = _____ millimeters

   f. 1 millimeter = _____ meters

2. Fill in the blanks.

   a. 2 m = _____ dm

   b. 5 m = _____ cm

   c. 8 m = _____ dm

   d. 1 m = _____ mm

   e. 7 m = _____ cm

   f. 9 dm = _____ m

   g. 9 mm = _____ m

   h. 8 cm = _____ m

   i. 6 dm = _____ m

3. Fill in the blanks.

   To change from meters to millimeters, add _____ zeros.

   To change from meters to decimeters, add _____ zeros.

   To change from meters to centimeters, add _____ zeros.

4. Which of these units (meters, centimeters, millimeters) would work best to measure?

   _____ a. width of a pencil lead

   _____ b. football field

   _____ c. crayon box

   _____ d. race at a track meet

5. Complete the following chart:

meter	decimeters	centimeters	millimeters
1 m	_____ dm	_____ cm	_____ mm

CHALLENGE:

The scientist, George Washington Carver, lived most of his life at Tuskegee Institute in Tuskegee, Alabama. He developed hundreds of uses for peanuts. Measure the length of this peanut in mm, cm and dm. _____ mm = _____ cm = _____ dm

LEVEL 4, METRIC SYSTEM

MATCHING

_____ 1. 1 meter   a. 1000 meters

_____ 2. 1 kilometer b. .01 meter

_____ 3. 1 decimeter c. .001 meter

_____ 4. 1 centimeter d. 10 decimeters

_____ 5. 1 millimeter e. .1 meter

Fill in the blanks.

6. 1 m = _____ dm

7. 1 km = _____ m

8. 1 m = _____ cm

9. 1 cm = _____ m

10. 1 m = _____ mm

11. 1 mm = _____ m

12. Fill in the blanks.

a. 6 m = _____ dm b. 7 cm = _____ m c. 13 mm = _____ m

d. 4 m = _____ mm e. 25 m = _____ cm f. 8 km = _____ m

g. 6 m = _____ dm h. 70 cm = _____ m i. 8 km = _____ m

13. There are about 2.5 centimeters in 1 inch. If a box is 5 inches wide, how wide is it in centimeters? _____

14. A meter is about 39.4 inches. If a room is 118.2 inches high, how high is it in meters? _____

15. How many inches in a yard? _____ In a meter? _____

16. Which is longer—100 yards or 100 meters? _____

CHALLENGE:

In Kentucky's Mammoth Cave, some of the chambers are large enough to hold a 12-story building. If a chamber is 120 feet high, how tall is it in meters? Round off. _____

LESSON PLAN 5: PERIMETER & CIRCUMFERENCE

OBJECTIVES: For all four levels.

1. Understand the concepts of perimeter, radius, diameter and circumference.
2. Continue to use the metric system in measurement.

(Note: If students need review on working with fractions or decimals, refer to *Math Phonics™—Fractions & Decimals*.)

MATH HISTORY: As early as 2000 B.C., Egyptians knew the distance around any circle was about three times the distance across. Now we know it is closer to $3^1/_7$ or 3.14, and we refer to this number as pi (pronounced pie). It is the Greek letter π and stands for "perimeter around the circle."

LEVEL 1: Use for third grade or as needed.

1. Introduce the term *perimeter*.
2. Calculate perimeters.
3. Continue to use metric units.

CLASSROOM PRESENTATION: Spend a few minutes discussing the term *perimeter*. Ask the class if any of them have heard someone in a western or war movie say: "We need to send one of the men to scout around the perimeter of camp." If so, what did this mean? It means scout around the outer edge of the camp. In geometry, the term means "the distance around some plane figure such as a square or rectangle." Draw this on the board:

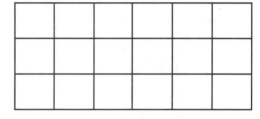

Each square is one foot. How many feet of fence would be needed to enclose this area?

$$6' + 3' + 6' + 3' = 18 \text{ feet}$$

If the figure is a square, you only need to know one side. The others are all the same. For a rectangle, opposite sides are equal.

$$9 + 4 + 9 + 4 = 26 \text{ m} \qquad 7 + 7 + 7 + 7 = 28 \text{ feet}$$
$$\text{or}$$
$$7 \times 4 = 28 \text{ feet}$$

9 m

4 m

7'

When you find perimeter, numbers are usually labeled as feet, inches, meters, etc. Always use the same label for the answer. The answer is wrong without the label.

TAKE-HOME: Worksheet Q, page 64.

OPTIONAL: Coloring Page, page 68.

LESSON PLAN 5: PERIMETER & CIRCUMFERENCE

LEVEL 2: Use for fourth grade or as needed. Review Level 1.

1. Discuss regular polygons.
2. Introduce radius and diameter.

CLASSROOM PRESENTATION:

Regular Polygons

A regular polygon has all its sides the same length. A square is always a regular polygon. If we know one side of a square, how can we find the perimeter?

5 meters

Add the four sides or multiply by 4.
5 + 5 + 5 + 5 = 20 meters. What is the perimeter of this regular polygon?

15 x 5 = 75 inches

15 inches

If you know one side of a regular polygon, you can multiply by the number of sides. (Go over this again for Level 3.)

RADIUS AND DIAMETER:

In any circle, the distance from the center to a point on the circle is called the *radius*.

The distance from one point on the circle to another point on the circle passing through the center is called the diameter. The diameter is always radius times two.

d = 18"

If the diameter is 18", what is the radius? (9")

TAKE-HOME: Worksheet R, page 65; Coloring Page, page 68.

OPTIONAL: Math Spelling Test
Spelling words: perimeter, radius, diameter, regular polygon

LEVEL 3: Use for fifth grade or as needed. Review if needed.

1. Demonstrate why pi is about $3^1/_7$.
2. Practice finding circumference.
3. Review perimeter of regular polygons.
4. Discuss how to find missing dimensions.

CLASSROOM PRESENTATION:

Circumference is from the same root word as *circle* and means "distance around a circle." Circumference of any circle is always about $3^1/_7$ times the distance across that same circle (diameter).

Do this demonstration to help students understand the meaning of pi and how to find circumference.

Cut two circles from tagboard. One should have a diameter of 7 inches. The other should have a diameter of 14 inches. (A 14-inch pizza cardboard works great.) Do this demonstration with the 7-inch circle.

1. Measure the circle with a ruler so the class will know the diameter is 7 inches.
2. Have a student hold the circle and wrap a piece of masking tape around the edge of the circle.
3. Put the masking tape on the board or a table and measure the length.
4. It should be about 22 inches. Now take pi times diameter.

$7 \times 3^1/_7 = {}^1\!7/_1 \times {}^{22}/_7{}_1 = 22$ inches (length of the tape)

Do the same with the 14-inch circle. Go over this again for the Level 4 presentation. Problems using this will be on the Level 4 worksheet.

MISSING DIMENSIONS:
If you know the perimeter of a figure, how do you find a missing dimension?

perimeter = 35'

```
 I I
 8      35
+ 7    - 26
 26     9 ft.
```

Add the dimensions you know. Subtract from the perimeter.

TAKE-HOME:
Worksheet S, page 66.

OPTIONAL:
Math Spelling Test
Spelling words: perimeter, regular polygon, radius, diameter, circumference, pi

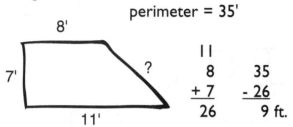

LEVEL 4:
Use for sixth grade or as needed. Review if needed.

1. Review the demonstration of pi, page 62.
2. Discuss finding the perimeter of a semicircle.
3. Discuss the perimeter of a semicircle connected to a square or rectangle.

CLASSROOM PRESENTATION:
Review the demonstration of the meaning of pi given in Level 3. Do the whole thing again if necessary. Tell students that pi can be $3\frac{1}{7}$ or 3.14, but we are only going to use $3\frac{1}{7}$ in this section.

If we know the radius, find the diameter with this formula:

$$2r = d$$

If we know the diameter, find the circumference with this formula:

$$\pi d = c \text{ or } 2\pi r = c$$

For a semicircle, find the circumference. Take half of that number. Then add the diameter for the flat side of the semicircle.

For example:

d = 14"

$$C = \pi d$$
$$= 3\tfrac{1}{7} \times 14$$
$$= {}^{22}/_7 \times {}^{14}/_1 = 44"$$

Half of 44" = 22"

```
  22
+ 14
```
perimeter = 36"

TAKE-HOME:
Worksheet T, page 67. Give each student a copy of Wall Chart 4 on page 69. Go over the explanation using r = 7"; d = 14" and c = 44". Students should keep this in their math notebooks for later reference.

OPTIONAL:
Math Spelling Test
Spelling words: perimeter, regular polygon, radius, diameter, circumference, pi, semicircle, dimension

LEVEL 1, PERIMETER

Find the perimeter in centimeters for each.

1. _____

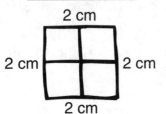

2 cm
2 cm   2 cm
2 cm

2. _____

5 cm

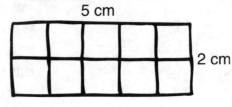

2 cm

3. _____

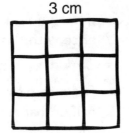

3 cm

4. _____

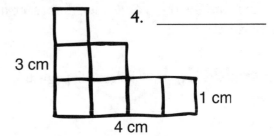

3 cm

1 cm

4 cm

Find the perimeter for each.

5. _____

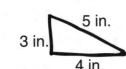

5 in.
3 in.
4 in.

6. _____

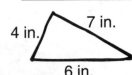

10 ft.
3 ft.

7. _____

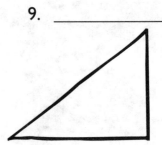

7 in.
4 in.
6 in.

Cut out the centimeter stick on this page. Measure these figures and find the perimeter.

8. _____

9. _____

REVIEW

10. a. 1 m = _____ cm   b. 500 cm = _____ m

11. Name a four-sided plane figure. _____

12. What is the name of the solid shaped like a soup can? _____

CHALLENGE:

The view from Colorado's Pikes Peak inspired Katherine Lee Bates to write "America, the Beautiful." Find the perimeter of the state of Colorado if it is 370 miles wide and 280 miles long.

Name _____

LEVEL 2, PERIMETER

Find the perimeter for each. The side of each small square is one centimeter.

1. _____

2. _____

3. _____

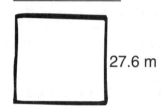

Find the perimeter for each square.

4. _____

5. _____

6. _____

39 in.

9³/₄ ft.

27.6 m

Find the missing dimension.

7. _____

8. _____

9. _____

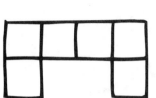
d = ? r = 4ft.

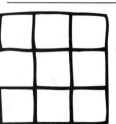
d = 15" r = ?

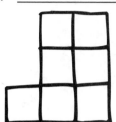
d = 7.9 m r = ?

10. Your family garden is a rectangle 8.9 m long and 7.6 m wide. What is the perimeter? _____

11. Find the perimeter of a regular pentagon with each side 12 meters long. _____

REVIEW

12. Name one line _____, one angle _____, one ray _____.

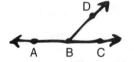

13. A centimeter is about the width of a _____ stick.

14. Which metric unit would you use (meter, kilometer or millimeter) to measure the width of a pencil lead? _____

CHALLENGE:

Wyoming is the home of Yellowstone National Park and the majestic Grand Teton mountains. It is also famous for giving women the right to vote in 1869. If the perimeter of Wyoming is 1328 miles, find the missing dimension, DC. _____

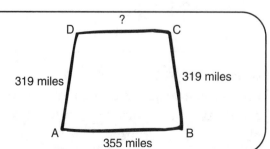

LEVEL 3, PERIMETER

Find the perimeter of these regular polygons.

1. _____

127.8 cm

2. _____

18⁷/₈ ft.

3. _____

29.83 in.

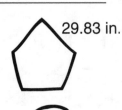

4. If the radius of a pizza is 8 inches, what is the diameter? _____   r = 8"

5. What is the radius of a flowerbed that is 4.2 meters in diameter? _____

   What is the radius in centimeters? _____

6. Find the length of the other side.

   a. $\overline{BC}$ = _____ perimeter = 194 ft.

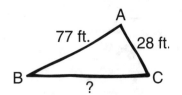

   b. $\overline{DG}$_____ perimeter = 279 m

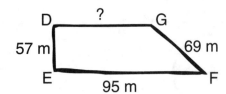

REVIEW

7. How many sides? a. ____ rhombus   b. ____ hexagon   c. ____ decagon   d. ____ quadrilateral
   e. ____ nonagon   f. ____ parallelogram

8. Fill in the blanks. I m = ____ cm = ____ mm = ____ dm

9 An angle smaller than a right angle is called _____.

10. An angle larger than a right angle is called _____.

11. Circle the right answer: If a solid has triangular sides which meet at one point, it is a
    (pyramid, prism).

CHALLENGE:
Kansas is a major producer of wheat and cattle and is the world leader in the manufacture of private
airplanes. If the perimeter of Kansas is about 1200 miles, what would it be in kilometers? (One mile is
about ⁸/₅ of a kilometer.)

Name _____

LEVEL 4, PERIMETER & CIRCUMFERENCE

Find the missing dimensions. Use pi = $3^1/_7$.

1. diameter = _____ circumference = _____   2. radius = _____ circumference = _____

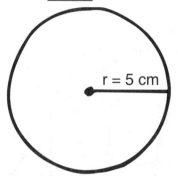

r = 5 cm

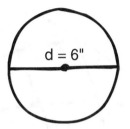

d = 6"

3. Find the perimeter. perimeter = _____   4. Find the perimeter. perimeter = _____

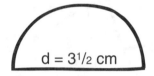

d = 3$^1/_2$ cm

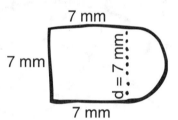

7 mm

7 mm

d = 7 mm

7 mm

5. Hawaii's most famous volcano is Mauna Loa. It is 3 miles across the base. What is the circumference of the base of the volcano? _____

REVIEW

6. Perpendicular lines form _____ angles.

7. Acute or obtuse: 30° _____; 120° _____

MATCHING

_____ 8. decimeter   a. width of a pencil lead

_____ 9. meter   b. height of a soup can

_____ 10. millimeter   c. about 39.4 inches

CHALLENGE:

If a meter is $^1/_{10,000,000}$ of the distance from the equator to the North Pole, what is the circumference of the Earth in meters? _____

MATH ART

This double spiraling pattern can be found in a nature in a daisy head.

AREA OF A CIRCLE

1. DIVIDE A CIRCLE INTO EIGHT PARTS.

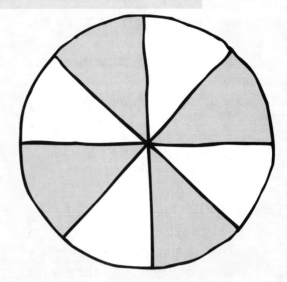

2. REARRANGE THE PARTS.

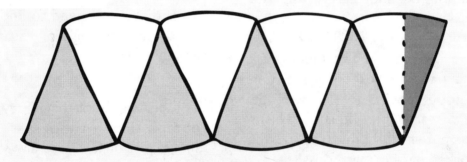

3. PUT THE SMALL TRIANGLE ON THE OTHER SIDE.

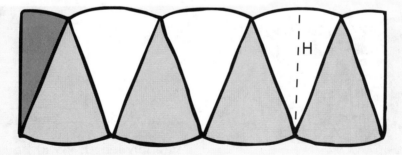

4. NOW WE HAVE "ALMOST" A RECTANGLE.

area of rectangle = base x height

height = radius of the circle or (r)

base = $\frac{1}{2}$ circumference ___

$\qquad$ $\frac{1}{2} (\pi \cdot D)$ or $(\pi \cdot \frac{1}{2}D)$ or $(\pi \cdot r)$

area = $\pi \cdot r \cdot r = \pi r^2$

LESSON PLAN 6: AREA & VOLUME

OBJECTIVES: For all four levels.

1. Understand the concepts of area and volume.
2. Develop the process of calculating area and volume.
3. See uses for area and volume in everyday situations.

MATH HISTORY:
Once again we see the Egyptians and Greeks excelling at finding areas and volumes. The Egyptians were especially good at finding areas of fields and volumes for piles of grain and buckets for carrying it. The Greeks had answers that were more precise, but the Egyptians were more skillful because of daily practice. In the Old Testament book of Genesis, the patriarch Joseph was put in charge of the food supplies for all of Egypt. The name *Joseph* means "may he add." This is an example of a person coming to power because he worked hard in math class!

LEVEL 1: Use for third grade or as needed.

1. Introduce the concept of finding area.
2. Discuss practical uses.

CLASSROOM PRESENTATION: Draw a 3 x 3 square grid on the board.

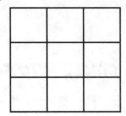

Imagine that this is an entry floor. If we were going to put wood trim around the edge, how many feet of trim would we need? (12 feet) That would be the perimeter. Now imagine that we will be putting one-foot square tiles down to cover it. How many tiles will be needed? (9) That would be the area.

To find area, we need to know the length and width of a rectangle or square. Then multiply length x width.

$$A = L \times W$$

The perimeter of that entry floor has a label of feet. However, for area, we need to say *square feet* or ft^2. Area always has a label with *square* as part of it.

What is the area of this field?

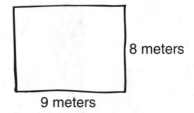

8 meters

9 meters

Multiply length x width.

72 square meters or 72 m^2.

TAKE-HOME: Worksheet U, page 73.

OPTIONAL: Math Art, page 77.

LEVEL 2: Use for fourth grade or as needed.

1. Introduce area of a right triangle.
2. Discuss area with a part missing.
3. Discuss volume.

CLASSROOM PRESENTATION: Put this rectangle on the board.

What is the area of this rectangle?

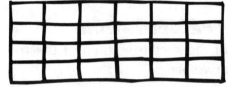

4 ft. x 6 ft.
24 ft.²

What is the area of this triangle?

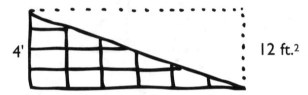

4'   12 ft.²

The triangular area is half of the rectangle.

To find the area of a triangle, use this formula:

$$A = \frac{1}{2} \times (L \times W)$$
$$A = \frac{1}{2} \times (4 \times 6)$$
$$A = \frac{1}{2} (24) = 12 \text{ ft.}^2$$

Examples:

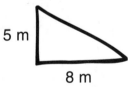

5 m
8 m

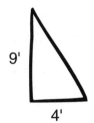

9'
4'

$A = \frac{1}{2} \times (5 \times 8)$ $A = \frac{1}{2} \times (9 \times 4)$
$A = \frac{1}{2} \times (40) = 20 \text{ ft.}^2$ $A = \frac{1}{2} \times (36) = 18 \text{ ft.}^2$

AREA WITH A MISSING PART: What is the area of this wall without the window? Find the area of the entire wall. Find the area of the window. Subtract.

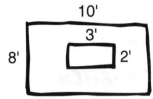

10'
3'
8'   2'

8 x 10 = 80
3 x 2 = 6
80 - 6 = 74 ft.²

Have the class do this sample problem.

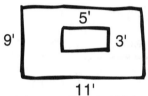

5'
9'   3'
11'

VOLUME: Sometimes it is necessary to measure the interior of a box or room. This measurement is called volume. If a box is one foot along each edge, it has volume of 1 cubic foot. Answers for volume problems have a label with the word *cubic* in them.

Draw this storage box on the board. To demonstrate this, use small tissue boxes. They are not exactly a cube, but they are close.

This storage unit measures 2 feet x 2 feet x 2 feet. How many cubic foot boxes can be placed in it? First, find out how many would be on the bottom layer. (4) How many layers would there be? (2) Total number of boxes? (8) To find the volume of a space, multiply L x W x H = V. Repeat this demonstration for Level 3.

TAKE-HOME: Worksheet V, page 74.

OPTIONAL: Math Spelling Test

Spelling words: perimeter, circumference, area, volume, cubic, square

LESSON PLAN 6: AREA & VOLUME

LEVEL 3: Use for fifth grade or as needed.

1. Review fractions and decimals as dimensions.
2. Review volume.

CLASSROOM PRESENTATION:

What is the area of this rectangle? When the length and width are not whole numbers, we still find area by multiplying.

4.5 m

3.2 m

$$A = L \times W$$
$$L = 3.2 \text{ m} \quad W = 4.5 \text{ m}$$

Recall that when you multiply numbers with decimals, you need to count decimal places and the answer has the same number of decimal places as in the problem. (For a wall chart which explains this, see page 55 in *Math Phonics™–Decimals*.)

```
  4.5
x 3.2
   90            14.4 m²
 135
14.40
```

Practice: L = 5.1 in.
W = 3.4 in.

```
  5.1
x 3.4
 204           17.34 in²
 153
17.34
```

What about 3¹/₂ in. x 2¹/₄ in.? First change to a mixed number and then multiply. (If students do not remember how to do this, see page 36 *Math Phonics™–Fractions & Decimals Bonus Book*.)

Review volume on Level 2.

TAKE-HOME: Worksheet W, page 75.

LEVEL 4: Use for sixth grade or as needed.

1. Teach area of a figure with more than one part.
2. Review volume.
3. Review finding area with a part missing.

CLASSROOM PRESENTATION:

Find the area of the rectangle, then of the triangle. Add the two areas.

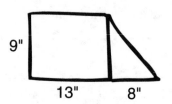

9"

13"   8"

Rectangle
$$A = 9 \times 13 = 117 \text{ in.}^2$$

```
  117
+  36
  153 in.²
```

Triangle
$$A = \tfrac{1}{2} \times (8 \times 9)$$
$$= \tfrac{1}{2} \times (72) = 36 \text{ in.}^2$$

Review volume on level 2.
Review area with a part missing on level 2.

TAKE-HOME: Worksheet X, page 76.

OPTIONAL: Math Spelling Test: same as Level 3

Name _____

LEVEL 1, AREA

Find the perimeter in centimeters. Find the area in square centimeters. (Each small square is 1cm on each side.)

1. perimeter = _____   area = _____

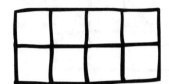

2. perimeter = _____   area = _____

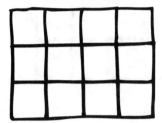

Find the perimeter and area for these rectangles.

3. perimeter = _____   area = _____

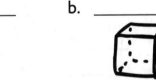

3'
6'

4. perimeter = _____   area = _____

4'
9'

REVIEW

5. One meter is about the distance from a _____ to the floor.

6. a. 5 m = _____ cm   b. 20 m = _____ cm

    c. 300 cm = _____ m   d. 15 m = _____ cm

7. Name these solids.

   a. _____   b. _____   c. _____   d. _____

8. Find the perimeter of these rectangles.

   a. _____   b. _____   c. _____

5 m
9 m

3 m
4 m

8 cm
2 cm

CHALLENGE:
How many small cubes are in this cube toy? _____

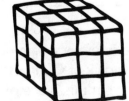

Name _____

LEVEL 2, AREA OF A TRIANGLE

Give the area in square centimeters.

1. area = _____

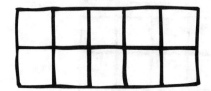

2. area = _____

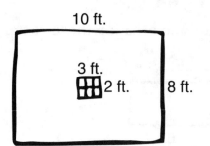

4 cm

4 cm

3. The school is going to paper this wall of your classroom. How many square feet of wallpaper will be needed? (There will be no wallpaper on the windows.) _____

10 ft.

3 ft.
2 ft.   8 ft.

4. This flowerbed is in three parts. What is the total area of the three parts? _____

8'

5'   12'   5'

REVIEW

5. Find the perimeter. a. _____ b. _____

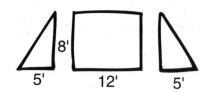

a.
3 m
3 m 7 m
6 m   3 m
10 m

b.
10 ⁷/₈ in.
5 ¹/₈ in.

6. Find the radius. _____

d = 3¹/₂'

7. Fill in the blanks. A nonagon has _____ sides; pentagon has _____ sides; parallelogram has _____ sides.

CHALLENGE:

New Hampshire granite is of very high quality and was used in building our country's Library of Congress. How many one-foot cubes of granite are there in this piece of granite? _____

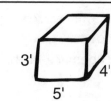

3'   4'
5'

Name _____

LEVEL 3, AREA & VOLUME

Find the area.

1. area = _____

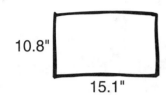

10.8"

15.1"

2. area = _____

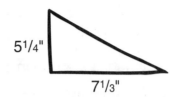

5¹/₄"

7¹/₃"

3. area = _____

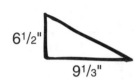

6¹/₂"

9¹/₃"

4. area = _____

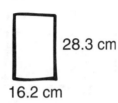

28.3 cm

16.2 cm

5. How many sugar cubes are in the top layer? _____

How many layers? _____

How many are in the box? _____

6. Find the volume of this block of steel.

area of base = _____

height = _____

volume = _____

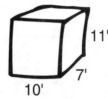

10'

12'

8'

7. How many one-foot cube boxes will fit into this cargo area in the back of a van? _____

11'

7'

10'

8. In the early years of the 20th century, the Wisconsin state legislature made it illegal to sell margarine in Wisconsin! Find the volume of this pound of butter. _____

2"

5"

2"

CHALLENGE:

North Carolina has the world's largest tobacco factories and is the country's largest manufacturer of household furniture. Find the volume of this cedar chest. _____

24.5"

41.3"   18.8"

LEVEL 4, AREA & VOLUME

1. One of the store windows in the mall is made up of a square part and a triangular part.

   What is the area of the entire window? _____

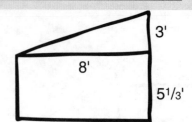

2. The store will be carpeting two rooms with these dimensions. One room has a small part cut away for an entry. How many square feet of carpeting will be needed in all? _____

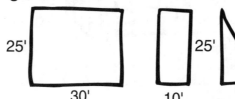

3. How many square feet of grass sod will be needed for these three patches of lawn? _____
   How many feet of fencing will be needed to enclose the three separate patches? _____

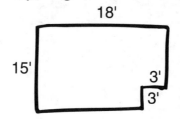

4. How many cubic feet of cement are needed for a concrete patio 10 feet by 12 feet and 2 feet thick? _____

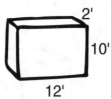

5. One of Idaho's natural wonders is Craters of the Moon National Monument. Its weird, twisted formations seem eerie to many people, but they are unique and unforgettable. Find the circumference of this crater. circumference = _____

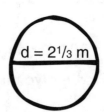

$d = 2\frac{1}{3}$ m

CHALLENGE:
Arkansas has the only diamond mine in North America. How many square inches of velvet would it take to cover all sides of this jewel box with no overlap? _____

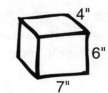

GEOMETRIC DESIGNS IN NATURE

This is a diagram of a single-celled, microscopic sea plant called a diatom. This plant is nearly a perfect circle and displays the symmetric beauty found in a stained glass window.

This is one of the designs found in the tourmaline, a semiprecious gem mined in Madagascar. Here we see a set of concentric triangles.

These interlocking cubes make up the crystalline structure of iron pyrite—commonly known as "fool's gold."

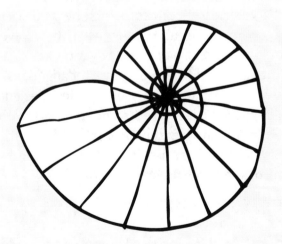

This is a cutaway sketch of a chambered nautilus seashell. The lines show the chambers for an equiangular spiral.

LESSON PLAN 7: LINES OF SYMMETRY & MEASURING ANGLES

OBJECTIVES: For all four levels.

1. Introduce the concept of symmetry.
2. Develop the process of measuring angles.

(Note: Understanding symmetry and the measure of angles will provide the foundation for the concept of congruent triangles—a vital component of many geometric proofs.)

MATH HISTORY: Ancient people struggled with the number of days in a calendar year, choosing numbers ranging from 354 to 365. As early as 3000 B.C., the Babylonians used 360 as the number of days in a year. The Egyptians and Mesopotamians did the same. Three hundred sixty-day calendars did not work over the long term, but the concept of a cycle being divided into 360 parts was still used for the number of degrees in a circle. Three hundred sixty has so many divisors that it is an excellent choice.

This is a fine example of the connection between a natural phenomena (the yearly cycle of seasons and how often they repeat) and a geometric concept which helps us organize so many areas of our lives. If we were unable to measure angles, navigation at sea and in the air would be much more dangerous. If we were unable to measure angles, designing buildings, vehicles, streets and gardens would pose a much greater problem. For other examples of geometric concepts found in nature, see the wall chart on page 77.

LEVEL 1: Use for third grade or as needed.

1. Introduce the concept of a line of symmetry.
2. Discuss figures having more than one line of symmetry.

CLASSROOM PRESENTATION: A line of symmetry is an imaginary line that divides a shape into two identical parts. Use a picture of a face and a small flat-edged mirror to demonstrate. If you place the mirror exactly halfway between the eyes, the face looks real. Moving the mirror to one side or the other makes it look strange but still the sides are congruent.

Have students trace, cut out and fold the top row of figures on Worksheet Y, page 81, to see that some lines form symmetry and some do not.

Have students experiment to see that some shapes have more than one line of symmetry. The triangle at the top of Worksheet Y has three although some triangles have none. The hexagon has six.

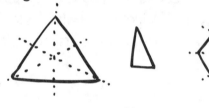

TAKE-HOME: Worksheet Y, page 81.

OPTIONAL: Use the flash cards on pages 14-15. Run off copies on paper. Let students cut out all the polygons and experiment with folding to find lines of symmetry. Give each student a copy of Wall Chart 5, page 77, and have students draw in lines of symmetry. Activity Page, page 48. Do the same.

LEVEL 2: Use for fourth grade or as needed. Review Level 1 if needed.

1. Develop the skill of drawing half of a symmetrical figure.
2. Introduce figures which are a reflection of each other.

CLASSROOM PRESENTATION:

Half of a Symmetrical Figure

Enlarge and laminate a piece of isometric dot paper. Draw these shapes and complete the other side so that the dotted line is a line of symmetry.

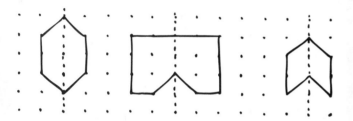

REFLECTIONS: Draw these sets of figures on the board.

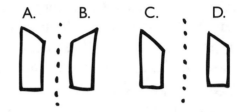

Figures A and B are reflections of each other. Figures C and D are the same shape but are not reflections of one another. Objects in a mirror are reversed—reflected figures are reversed.

Give each student a page of isometric dot paper. Give these instructions:

1. Fold the paper down the center. Draw a line of symmetry along the fold.
2. Draw a figure on one side of the fold. Count the dots to locate corners for the figure.
3. Draw the reflection on the opposite side of the fold line.

TAKE-HOME: Worksheet Z, page 82.

OPTIONAL: Give homework points for the drawing on the isometric dot paper—five points for getting the shapes identical and in the right location; up to five extra points for more detailed shapes and for neatness.

LEVEL 3: Use for fifth grade or as needed.

1. Practice measuring angles and copying angles of the same size.
2. Introduce hexagon flowers.

CLASSROOM PRESENTATION: Use the enlarged protractor, page 47, or a large wooden classroom protractor to demonstrate measuring an angle. If students have their own protractors, use those. If they do not, have them cut out the one at the bottom of Worksheet AA, page 83.

Draw a large 90° angle on the board. Explain these steps:

1. Place the vertex of the angle at the dot in the center of the protractor.
2. Place one of the rays so that it will pass through 0 on the protractor.
3. Look to see where the other ray passes through the number line on the protractor. That number tells how many degrees are in the angle. Two angles can have the same number of degrees even though one may have short rays and the other may have long rays.

Now draw angles of 30°, 100° and 75°. Have students practice with their protractors at their desks.

TAKE-HOME: Worksheet AA, page 83.

OPTIONAL: If students are having trouble understanding, give each student a copy of page 47, the large protractor and a vinyl page protector. Use a crayon or dry-erase marker to draw rays. Demonstrate drawing one ray from the center point through zero and the other ray through 70 for a 70° angle. Try other sizes of angles.

Activity Page—Hexagon Flowers Without a Compass, page 85.

LEVEL 4: Use for sixth grade or as needed. Review if needed.

1. Practice drawing angles of a given measure.
2. Discuss symmetry in nature.

CLASSROOM PRESENTATION: Draw angles on the board and let students take turns measuring them with the wooden or laminated protractor. Give students a large protractor and vinyl page protector for practice at their desks. Give them a number of degrees to draw on their own papers.

Discuss Wall Chart 4—Geometric Designs in Nature, page 77. Many of our beautiful buildings and artwork reflect designs that exist in the natural world.

TAKE-HOME: Worksheet BB, page 84.

OPTIONAL: Math Art—Making Curves from Straight Lines, page 86. Students can design different curves from straight lines on a plain piece of dot paper, pages 19-20.

Name _____

LEVEL 1, LINES OF SYMMETRY

Trace these shapes on paper and cut them out. Fold on the dotted line to see if it is a line of symmetry.

 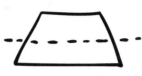

Is the dotted line a line of symmetry?

1. _____ 2. _____ 3. _____

 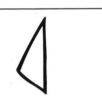

How many lines of symmetry in the shapes below?

4. _____ 5. _____ 6. _____ 7. _____

 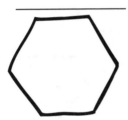 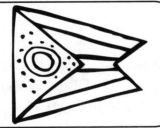

REVIEW

8. Find the perimeter. _____

   Find the area. _____

10 m

7 m [rectangle] 7 m

10 m

MATCHING

9. ____ 1 meter   a. about the width of a craft stick

   ____ 1 centimeter   b. about the height of a soup can

   ____ 1 decimeter   c. about the distance from a doorknob to the floor

10. a. 1 m = _____ dm   d. 500 cm = _____ m

    b. 1 m = _____ cm   e. 3 m = _____ cm

    c. 100 cm = _____ m   f. 8 m = _____ cm

CHALLENGE:

Ohio is one of the richest manufacturing states in the country. It produces tires, aircraft, jet engines and ice cream cones, to name a few. The state also gave us seven Presidents. Find a line of symmetry in the Ohio state flag.

LEVEL 2, LINES OF SYMMETRY

Is the dotted line a line of symmetry? Yes or no for each. Draw in any other lines of symmetry.

1. _____   2. _____   3. _____   4. _____

How many lines of symmetry?

5. _____   6. _____   7. _____   8. _____

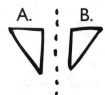   3   H   A

Draw the other half of each figure so that the dotted line is a line of symmetry.

9.   10.   11.   12.

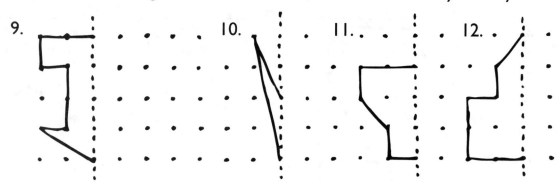

13. Figure A is a reflection of Figure B. Draw a reflection of Figure C so that the dotted line is a line of symmetry. Do the same for Figure E.

    A.   B.   C.   D.   E.   F.

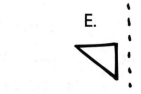

14. On the back of this page, write all the capital letters that have one or more lines of symmetry. Make all the real words you can think of from those letters. Draw lines of symmetry.

CHALLENGE:

The country's oldest European settlement was started in 1565 at St. Augustine, Florida. The city still stands today—complete with an authentic castle, moat and drawbridge from the 1500s. (Oh yes, Florida is also the home of DisneyWorld and Kennedy Space Center.) Draw all the lines of symmetry in the Florida state flag.

LEVEL 3, SYMMETRY & MEASURING ANGLES

How many lines of symmetry: 0, 1 or 2? Draw in the lines.

1. _____   2. _____   3. _____   4. _____

5. Cut out the protractor at the bottom of the page. Cut out the center so you can see the rays of the angles. Measure these angles. Write down the number of degrees.

a. _____   b._____   c. _____   d. _____

 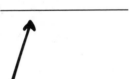  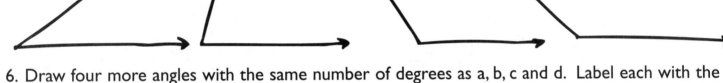

6. Draw four more angles with the same number of degrees as a, b, c and d. Label each with the same letter as its matching angle.

a.   b.   c.   d.

REVIEW

7. Draw lines of symmetry.

a.   b.   c.   d.

8. Draw the reflection of each figure.

a.   b.

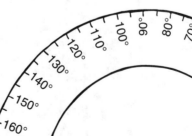

Name _____

LEVEL 4, MEASURING ANGLES

Measure these angles. Write down the number of degrees.

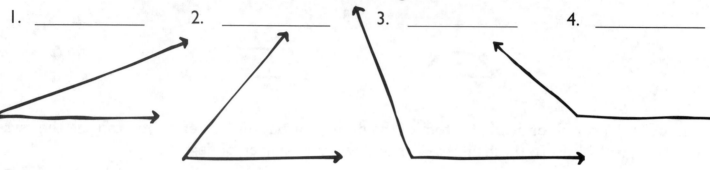

1. _____

2. _____

3. _____

4. _____

Draw angles with the given measure.

5. 90°

6. 75°

7. 120°

8. 43°

9. 138°

10. 180°

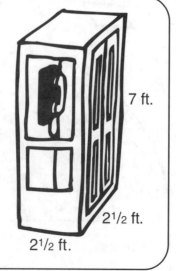

CHALLENGE:
Connecticut claims a lot of firsts in this country: first newspaper, insurance company, law school, dictionary, public art museum, use of anesthesia and the first public pay phone. Find the volume of this phone booth.

Volume = _____

7 ft.

2½ ft.

2½ ft.

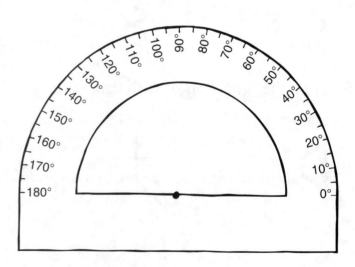

HEXAGON FLOWERS WITHOUT A COMPASS

Figure 1

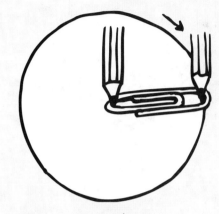

Materials: 1 paper clip, perferrably 1⁷/₈" long
2 pencils—one very sharp
1 piece of paper or 4" x 6" index card
folded paper towel or several pieces of paper for padding

Step 1: Put the padding under your paper or index card.

Step 2: Arrange the pencils and paper clip with the sharp pencil at the center of where the flower will be located. Poke the sharp pencil through the paper and move the other pencil around in a complete circle. (Figure 1)

Figure 2

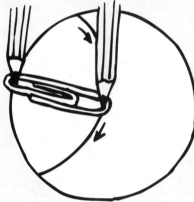

Step 3: Now move the pointed pencil to a point on the circle and draw an arc across the interior of the circle. (Figure 2)

Step 4: Move the pointed pencil to the end of the arc and draw another arc. (Figure 3)

Figure 3

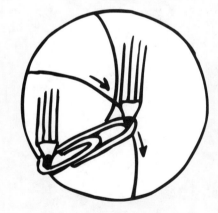

Step 5: Repeat step 3 until you have six arcs which form a flower. (Figure 4)

Step 6: See what other designs you can make this way. Fill a page and color for an art project.

Figure 4

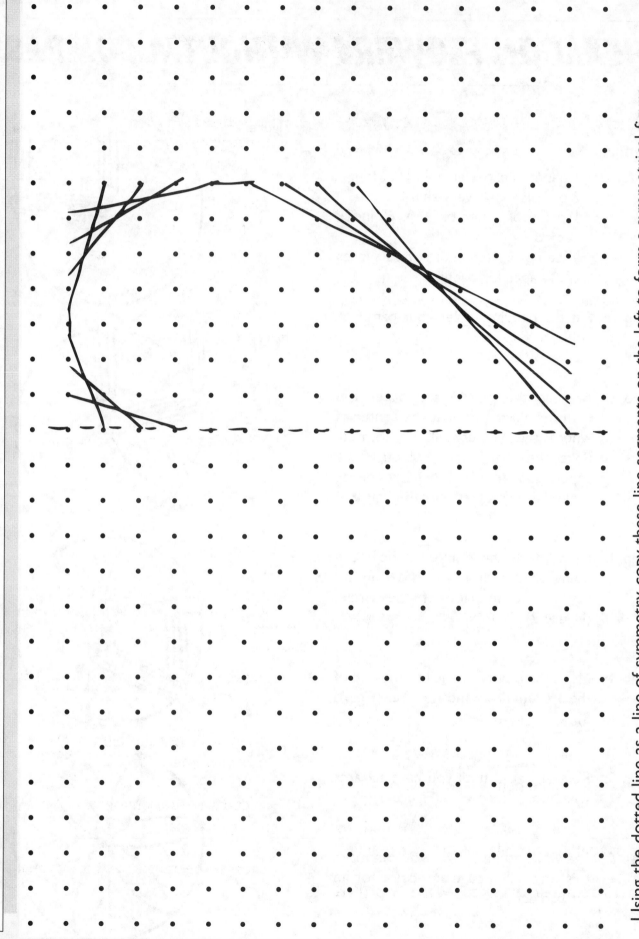

Using the dotted line as a line of symmetry, copy these line segments on the left to form a symmetrical figure. (Note: Sometimes architects and car designers form the outline of a curve by using a series of straight lines.)

Name _____

SUMMARY

SOLIDS: THREE-DIMENSIONAL FIGURES

curved surfaces—cone, sphere, hemisphere

flat surfaces—prisms, pyramids

pyramid—solid shape with a polygon base and triangular sides which meet at one point. Polygon base names the pyramid.

prism—solid shape with congruent polygon top and base and rectangular sides. Polygon base names the prism.

rectangular solid—prism with all rectangular sides

cube—prism with all equal edges and right angles

closed plane figures—triangle, rectangle, square, circle. A circle is not a polygon.

non-closed plane figure—letter C or S

polygon—closed plane figure formed by line segments (triangle, rectangle, square)

quadrilateral—four sides—Clue word is *quarter*.

other plane figures—

pentagon—five-sided polygon, (The Department of Defense building)

hexagon—six-sided polygon (X as in the number six.)

heptagon—seven-sided polygon (September was once the seventh month.)

octagon—eight-sided polygon (Clue word is *octopus*.)

nonagon—nine-sided polygon (Non is similar to nine.) See the pictures on the flash cards on pages 14-15.

decagon—10-sided polygon (Clue word is *decade*.) See the pictures on the flash cards on pages 14-15.

quadrilateral—any four-sided polygon

trapezoid—two sides parallel; two sides not parallel (Clue: picture a trapeze.)

parallelogram—four sides; opposite sides parallel

rhombus—parallelogram with four equal sides   or

rectangle—parallelogram with four right angles

square—rectangle with four equal sides

POINTS, LINES, PLANES, ANGLES

line segment—section of a straight line with two endpoints

A●———●B

intersection—point where two segments cross

ray—part of a line that has one endpoint and extends in one direction without end

A   B

angle—two rays with the same endpoint

A
B

protractor—curved number line used for measuring angles

90°
180°   0°

right angle—90° angle

acute angle—angle measuring less than 90°

obtuse angle—angle measuring more than 90°

perpendicular lines—two lines which intersect and form four right angles

degrees—used for measuring angles; 360° in a circle

METRIC SYSTEM

meter—about the distance from a doorknob to the floor; about 39.4 inches

decimeter—about the height of a soup can; about four inches

centimeter—about the width of a craft stick; about $1/2$ inch

millimeter—about the width of a pencil lead

1 meter = 10 decimeters (decade) = 100 centimeters (century) = 1000 millimeters (millennium)

kilometer—1000 meters; used like miles

PERIMETER, CIRCUMFERENCE, DIAMETER, RADIUS, AREA, VOLUME, SYMMETRY

4'
3'   3'
4'

perimeter—distance around a figure

perimeter = 4 + 3 + 4 + 3 = 14'

circumference—distance around a circle

pi (π)—about $3 1/7$; circumference of any circle is about $3 1/7$ times the diameter.

C = 7 x $3^1/_7$ ^{1}/₁ x ^{22}/₇ = 22"

d = 7"

diameter—distance across a circle through the center

radius—distance from the center of a circle to a point on the circle

d
r

2 x r = d

area—area of a square or rectangle is length times width

A = 3 x 4 = 12 ft.²

W = 3'
L = 4'

area of a triangle—$1/2$ base times height

A = $1/2$ (3 x 4) = 6 ft.

3'
4'

volume—number of cubic units needed to fill a solid figure

volume of a prism—length times width times height

3 x 3 x 3 = 27 in.³

3"
3"
3"

line of symmetry—a line that divides a figure into two same-shaped figures

Name _____

LEVEL 1 ASSESSMENT

1. Name each solid or plane figure.

a. _____   b. _____   c. _____   d. _____

2. Give each clue word. a. _____ octagon b. _____ decagon c. _____ trapezoid

   d. _____ quadrilateral

3. Circle each line segment.

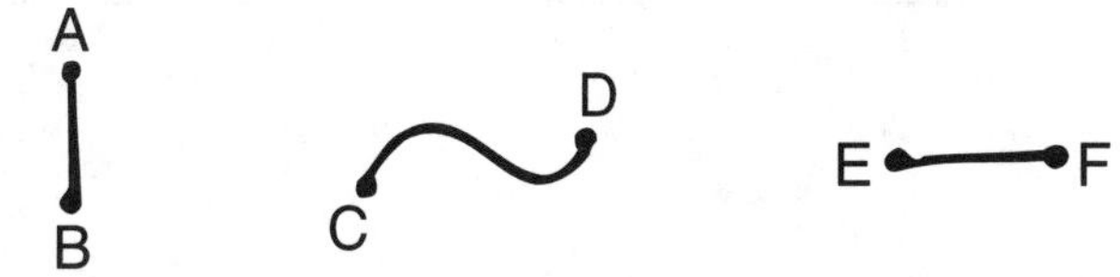

4. Name this segment. ____   X •———• Y

5. Fill in the blanks. A meter is about as long as the distance from a _____ to the floor. A centimeter is about the width of a _____ _____.

6. Find each perimeter. (Each small box is one inch on a side.)

   a. _____   b. _____   c. _____

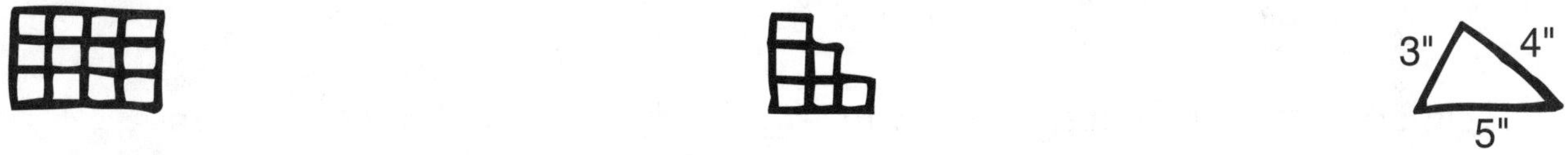

   3" 4"
   5"

7. Find the area of each square.

   a. _____   b. _____   c. _____

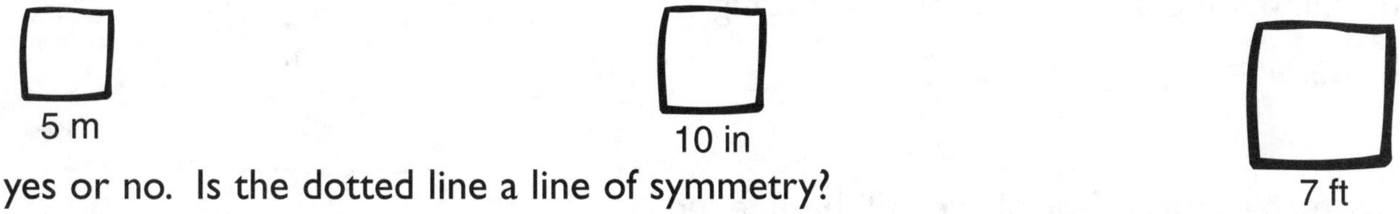

   5 m   10 in   7 ft

8. Write yes or no. Is the dotted line a line of symmetry?

   a. _____   b. _____   c. _____   d. _____

9. Draw all lines of symmetry.

   B   H   △   ▱   ♡

10. How many surfaces does a cube have? _____

LEVEL 2 ASSESSMENT

1. Name each solid.

a. _____ b._____ c._____ d. _____

2. Name each plane figure.

a. _____ b._____ c._____ d. _____

3. Give each clue word. a. _____ decagon b. _____ quadrilateral c. _____ hexagon

4. Name one line ____, one ray ____ and one angle ____.

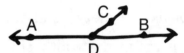

5. Draw a right angle. Label it angle ABC.

6. 100 decimeters = ____ meters   3 m = ____ dm   500 cm = ____ m

7. About how high is a decimeter? _____

8. Find the perimeter and area of this rectangle.

   perimeter = _____   area = _____

11.3 m

29.5 m

9. How many square feet of tile will be needed
   to cover this area with the center covered with
   carpet, not tile? _____

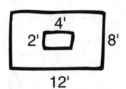

4'
2'   8'
12'

10. What is the diameter of a circle with a radius of 12 feet?   diameter = _____

11. Draw the reflection of this figure.

Name _____

LEVEL 3 ASSESSMENT

MATCHING

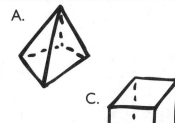

A.   B.   C.   D.

1. triangular prism _____
2. triangular pyramid _____
3. rectangular prism _____
4. rectangular pyramid_____

5. How many sides on a triangular prism? _____   How many vertices on a cube? _____

DEFINE

6. polygon: _____

7. pentagon:_____

8. hexagon: _____

9. acute angle: _____

10. obtuse angle: _____

11. a. 500 cm = _____ m   b. 10 m = _____ cm   c. 10 m = _____ mm

    d. 80 dm =_____ m   e. 9 mm = _____ m   f. 9 dm = _____ m

12. Find the missing dimension. perimeter = 280 cm

    missing dimension = _____

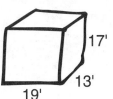

?
65 cm
58 cm
99 cm

13. What is the radius of a round flowerbed with a diameter of 125.8 feet? radius = _____

14. Find the volume of this block of steel.   volume = _____

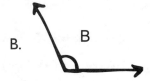

17'
13'
19'

15. Draw all lines of symmetry.

3 M N △

16. Which angle is about 30°? _____

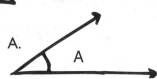

A.   B.

A   B

17. Draw a right angle. Label it angle ABC.

LEVEL 4 ASSESSMENT

1. Name each solid.

   a. _____   b. _____   c. _____

2. How many vertices in each? a. ____   b. ____   c. ____

DEFINE

3. prism: _____

4. pyramid: _____

5. polygon: _____

6. heptagon: _____

7. nonagon: _____

8. perpendicular lines: _____

9. a. 8 km = _____ m   b. 3000 mm = _____ m   c. 10 dm = _____ m

10. Find the missing dimensions.

    radius = _____

    circumference = _____

    d = 30"

11. Find the perimeter.   perimeter = _____

    d = 49 m

12. Find the area.   area = _____

    12'   9'

    9'

13. Find the volume.   volume = _____

    8.3"

    7"

    9"

14. Find the perimeter of a regular octagon with a side of 138.6 feet.   perimeter = _____

15. Draw all lines of symmetry.

   8   M

Worksheet A, page 17

1. cone
2. cone
3. cube or rectangular solid
4. rectangular solid
5. cylinder
6. hemisphere
7. sphere
8. cube
9. rectangular solid

10.

	sphere	cube	cylinder	cone	hemi-sphere	rectangu-lar solid
curved	1	0	1	1	1	0
flat	0	6	2	1	1	6

Challenge: rectangular solid

Worksheet B, page 18

1. sphere
2. cone
3. cube
4. cylinder
5. prism
6. pyramid

	7.	8.	9.	10.	11.
surfaces	6	4	5	5	8
edges	12	6	8	9	18
corners	8	4	5	6	12

Challenge:

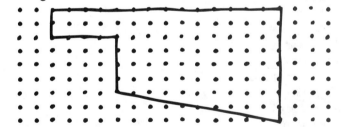

Worksheet C, page 21

1. D
2. A
3. B
4. C
5. Vertices: A. 8; B. 4; C. 5; D. 6
6. polyhedron: solid object whose sides are flat surfaces
7. cylinder: solid object having two flat surfaces and one curved surface
8. A. B. C.

Challenge: pentagonal pyramid

Worksheet D, page 22

1. rectangular prism or rectangular solid
2. cone
3. cylinder
4. triangular pyramid
5. rectangular pyramid
6. prism
7.

	1	2	3	4	5	6
flat surface	6	2	5	1	4	5
curved surface	0	1	0	1	0	0
edges	12	2	8	1	6	9
vertices	8	0	5	1	4	6

8. pyramid (See page 11 definitions.)
9. prism (See page 11 definitions.)
10. rectangular pyramid
11. triangular prim

Challenge:  Students should have a model on dot paper and a second one like this twice as large.

Worksheet E, page 33

1. b
2. a
3. c
4.-6. (See page 31.)
7. b
8. a
9. d
10. c
11. 6
12. sphere
13. cylinder

Challenge: square: 1; triangle: 4; rectangle: 2; circle: 1

Worksheet F, page 34

1. c
2. d
3. e
4. a
5. b
6.-9. (See page 31.)
10. a, b, c, e, f
11. a, b, e, f
12. b, f, e
13. b, f
14. 12
15. 8

Challenge: It's like a pyramid with the top cut off; trapezoid; the front is a trapezoid, but a trapezoid has no thickness. Neither name is perfect. Consider either answer okay.

Worksheet G, page 35

1.-4. (See page 31.)
5. c
6. d
7. a
8. b
9.-10. (See page 31.)
11. a, b, d, e
12. b, d, e
13. b, d, e
14. b, e
15. b
16. 8
17. triangular prism

Challenge: 8, 12, 6, 1

Worksheet H, page 36

1.-9. See pages 31-32.
10. c
11. a
12. b
13. circle
14. sphere
15. Pentagon
16. pyramid
17. prism
Challenge: cone and sphere or hemisphere

Worksheet I, page 43

1. $\overline{XY}$; $\overline{QR}$; $\overline{CD}$
2. $\overline{AB}$ or $\overline{BA}$
   A and B
3. $\overline{KL}$; $\overline{LM}$; $\overline{MK}$
4. W
5. a. 3; b. 4, c. 6, d. 5
6. a. cylinder; b. sphere; c. cone; d. rectangular solid
7. a. triangle; b. circle; c. trapezoid; d. rectangle
8. c—decagon, b—octagon, a—quadrilateral
Challenge: four segments

Worksheet J, page 44

1. $\overrightarrow{BA}$; $\overrightarrow{BC}$
2. $\angle DEF$; $\angle FED$; $\angle E$
3. $\overleftrightarrow{ML}$, $\overleftrightarrow{NK}$ or $\overleftrightarrow{MO}$, $\overleftrightarrow{NO}$ or $\overleftrightarrow{OL}$, $\overrightarrow{OK}$, $\angle MON$; $\angle NOL$; $\angle LOK$; $\angle KOM$
4. $\angle XYZ$ or $\angle ZYX$ or $\angle Y$; larger = $\angle A$; smaller = $\angle H$
5. Measure angle
6. a. 4, b. 3, c. 8, d. 10, e. 5, f. 4
7. b—pyramid, a—prism
Challenge: Rectangular prism or rectangular solid

Worksheet K, page 45

1. $\angle DAB$ or $\angle BAD$ also $\angle CAE$ or $\angle EAC$
2. $\angle EAB$ or $\angle BAE$ also $\angle CAD$ or $\angle DAC$
3. $\angle BAC$ or $\angle CAB$
4. acute: $\angle A$, $\angle E$, $\angle P$, obtuse: $\angle G$, $\angle K$, $\angle N$
5. Look at figure.
6. c
7. e
8. b
9. f
10. g
11. d
12. a
Challenge: rectangles = 4; squares = 1
Each section is a rectangle, the entire flag is a rectangle, The two sections at the right form a square.

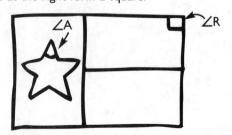

Worksheet L, page 46

1. acute: a, b, e   obtuse: c, d, f
2. $\overleftrightarrow{CF}$ and $\overleftrightarrow{AD}$
3. c
4. d
5. a
6. b
7. f
8. e
10. 360°
11. 8, 5, 6, 9, 4
Challenge: hexagons

Worksheet M, page 57

1. b
2. a
3. b. 500 cm, c. 900 cm, d. 1000 cm, e. 3 m, f. 4 m, g. 7 m, h. 8 m
4. a. yes, b. no, c. yes, d. no
5. Answers will vary.
6. 6
7. circle
8. $\overline{BA}$ or $\overline{AB}$
Challenge: meters

Worksheet N, page 58

1. doorknob
2. craft stick
3. soup can
4. 500 cm
5. 30 dm
6. 900 cm
7. .3
8. .07
9. 20 dm
10. 12 dm
11. Answers will vary.
12. Answers will vary.
13. no
14. $\overleftrightarrow{ON}$, or $\overrightarrow{NO}$, $\overrightarrow{ON}$
15. cylinder
16. pentagon
17. decagon
Challenge: 22 cm x 28 cm; .22 m x .28 m

Worksheet O, page 59

1. a. 10 dm; b. .1 m; c. 100 cm; d. .01 m; e.1000 mm; f. .001 m
2. a. 20 dm; b. 500 cm; c. 80 dm; d. 1000 mm; e. 700 cm; f. .9 m; g. .009 m; h. .08 m; i. .6 m
3. 3 zeros; 1 zero; 2 zeros
4. a. mm; b. m; c. mm or cm; d. m
5. 10 dm = 100 cm = 1000 m
Challenge: 25 mm = 2.5 cm = .25 dm

Worksheet P, page 60

1. d
2. a
3. e
4. b
5. c
6. 10dm
7. 1000m
8. 100cm
9. .01m
10. 1000mm
11. .001m
12. a. 60 dm, b. .07 m, c. .013 m, d. 4000 mm; e. 2500 cm, f. 8000 m; g. 60 dm, h. .7 m; i. 8000 m
13. 12.5 cm
14. 3 m
15. 36; 39.4
16. 100 meters
Challenge: 36.51 m or 36.5 m or 37 m

Worksheet Q, page 64

1. 8 cm
2. 14 cm
3. 12 cm
4. 14 cm
5. 12 in.
6. 26 ft.
7. 17 in.
8. 16 cm
9. 12 cm
10. a. 100 cm, b. 5 m
11. square, rectangle, parallelogram, rhombus or trapezoid
12. cylinder
Challenge: 1300 miles

Worksheet R, page 65

1. 14 cm
2. 14 cm
3. 12 cm
4. 156 in.
5. 39 ft.
6. 110.4 m
7. 8 ft.
8. $7\frac{1}{2}$ or 7.5 in.
9. 3.95 m or 4 m
10. 33 m
11. 60 m
12. $\overleftrightarrow{AB}$ or $\overleftrightarrow{AC}$ or $\overleftrightarrow{BC}$; $\angle ABD$ or $\angle DBA$ or $\angle DBC$ or $\angle CBD$; $\overrightarrow{BA}$ or $\overrightarrow{BC}$ or $\overrightarrow{BD}$
13. craft
14. millimeter
Challenge: 335 miles

Worksheet S, page 66

1. 511.2 cm
2. $113\frac{1}{4}$ ft.
3. 149.15 in.
4. d = 16 in.
5. 2.1 m; 210 cm
6. a. 89 ft., b. 58 m

7. a. 4, b. 6, c. 10, d. 4, e. 9, f. 4
8. 100; 1000; 10
9. acute
10. obtuse
11. pyramid
Challenge: 1920 km

Worksheet T, page 67

1. d = 10 cm; c = $31\frac{3}{7}$ cm
2. r = 3 in.; c = $18\frac{6}{7}$ in.
3. 9 cm
4. 32 mm
5. $9\frac{3}{7}$ miles
6. right or 90°
7. acute; obtuse
8. b
9. c
10. a
Challenge: 40,000,000 meters

Worksheet U, page 73

1. p = 12 cm; a = 8 cm²
2. p = 14 cm; a = 12 cm²
3. p = 18 ft.; a = 18 ft.²
4. 26 ft.; a = 36 ft.²
5. doorknob
6. a. 5 m = 500 cm; b. 20 m = 2000 cm; c. 300 cm = 3 m; d. 15 m = 1500 cm
7. a. sphere; b. cube; c. cylinder; d. cone
8. a. 28 m; b. 14 m; c. 20 cm
Challenge: 27

Worksheet V, page 74

1. a = 10 cm²
2. 8 cm²
3. 74 ft.²
4. 136 ft.²
5. a. p = 32 m; b. 32 in.
6. $1\frac{3}{4}$ ft.
7. 9; 5; 4
Challenge: 60 one-foot cubes

Worksheet W, page 75

1. 163.08 sq. in. or in.²
2. $19\frac{1}{4}$ in.² or sq. in.
3. $30\frac{1}{3}$ sq. ft.
4. 458.46 cm² or sq. cm
5. 18; 3; 54 sugar cubes
6. 960 cu. ft.
7. 770 foot cube boxes
8. 20 cu. in.
Challenge: 19022.78 cu. in.

Worksheet X, page 76

1. $54\frac{2}{3}$ sq. ft.
2. 441 ft.²
3. 1168 sq. ft.; 245 ft. of fencing
4. 240 cu. ft.
5. $7\frac{1}{3}$ m
Challenge: 188 square inches of velvet

Worksheet Y, page 81

1. yes
2. yes
3. yes
4. two lines
5. six lines
6. two lines
7. zero lines
8. 34 m; 70 m²
9. c; a; b
10. a. 10 dm, b. 100 cm, c. 1 m, d. 5 m, e. 300 cm, f. 800 cm

Challenge:

Worksheet Z, page 82

1. yes
2. no
3. no
4. no
5. none
6. one
7. two

Challenge:

8. one
9.   10.
11.   12.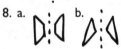
13. Refer to page 79.
14. ABCDEHIKMOSTU-VWXYZ; DEED; MOM; WOW; BOB; DID; TOT

Worksheet AA, page 83

1. 1   2. 1   3. zero   4. 2

5. a. 35°, b. 73°, c. 124°, d. 137°
6. Measure each student's angles
7. a.   b.   c. none   d.

8. a.   b.

Worksheet BB, page 84

1. 20°
2. 50°
3. 110°
4. 140°
5.-10. Check students' angles on all angle measurements. Allow two to three degrees error because of differences in pencil lead and protractors.

Challenge: 43¾ cu. ft.

Level 1 Assessment, page 89

1. a. cube; b. cone; c. rectangle; d. circle
2. a. octopus; b. decade; c. trapeze; d. quarter
3. $\overline{AB}$; $\overline{EF}$
4. $\overleftrightarrow{XY}$ or $\overleftrightarrow{YX}$
5. doorknob, craft stick
6. a. 14 in.; b. 12 in.; c. 12 in.
7. a. 25 m²; b. 100 in.²; 49 ft.²
8. a. no; b. no; c. yes; d. no
9.

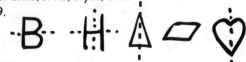

10. 6

Level 2 Assessment, page 90

1. a. triangular prism; b. cylinder; c. cube; d. rectangular pyramid
2. a. rectangle; b. pentagon; c. triangle; d. circle
3. a. decade; b. quarter; c. six
4. $\overleftrightarrow{AD}$ or $\overleftrightarrow{AB}$ or $\overleftrightarrow{DB}$; $\overleftrightarrow{DC}$; ∠ADC or ∠BDC
5. Measure angle.
6. 1 meter; 30 dm; 5 m
7. as high as a soup can
8. p = 81.6 m; a = 333.35 m²
9. 88 sq. ft.
10. d = 24 ft.
11. See page 79.

Level 3 Assessment, page 91

1. B
2. D
3. C
4. A
5. 4; 6
6. polygon: closed figure made of line segments
7. pentagon: five-sided polygon
8. hexagon: six-sided polygon
9. acute angle: angle less than 90°
10. obtuse angle: angle more than 90°
11. a. 5 m; b. 1000 cm; c. 10,000 mm; d. 8 m; e. .009 m; f. .9 m
12. 58 cm
13. 62.9 ft.
14. 4199 ft.³
15.

16. A
17. Measure angle.

Level 4 Assessment, page 92

1. a. triangular pryamid; b. cylinder; c. cube
2. a. 4; b. 0; c. 8
3. prism: solid object with polygon top and base and rectangular sides
4. pyramid: solid shape with polygon base and triangular sides which meet at one point
5. polygon: closed plane figure with line segments as sides
6. heptagon: seven-sided polygon
7. nonagon: nine-sided polygon
8. perpendicular lines: two lines which intersect to form four right angles
9. a. 8000 m; b. 3 m; c. 1 m
10. r = 15 in.; c = 94²/₇ in.
11. p = 126 m
12. a = 148.5 sq. ft.
13. v = 522.9 cu. in.
14. 1108.8 ft.
15.

TLC10406 Copyright © Teaching & Learning Company, Carthage, IL 62321-0010